INTERMEDIATE LOAN

THIS ITEM MAY BE BORROWED ~~~

ONE WEEK

INTERMEDIATE LOANS ARE IN HEAVY DEMAND,
PLEASE RETURN OR RENEW

To renew, telephone:
01243 816089 (Bishop Otter)
01243 812099 (Bognor Regis)

1 8 NOV 2005

2 7 MAY 2006

2 6 SEP 2006

3 0 NOV 2006

1 3 DEC 2006
2 5 MAY 2007

2 9 MAY 2007

1 5 DEC 2009
2 6 MAY 2011

Instant On Camera

The Fast Track To
Programme-making

Harris Watts

4

First published in 2004 by Aavo
8 Edis Street, London NW1 8LG
UK Copyright © 2004 Harris Watts
The moral right of the author has been asserted

ISBN 09507582 9 9

Illustrations by Brian Reading
Cover Design by Luke Westendarp
Desktop Publishing by Red Gables Facilities, Greenford
Printed by Lontec Print, St Albans

For Amy, Lucy, Matthew, Jonathan and Christina

My thanks to Roy Hanney, Justin Aggett and Heather Green for reading and commenting on parts of the text; and to Jenny Williams for her painstaking proof-reading. And special thanks to Marc Allen, Philippa Collins, Andrew Bonner and Dick Hammett for their detailed professional help.

The author, Harris Watts, has worked as a director and producer of current affairs and science documentaries (mainly for the BBC); as production manager for Brunei Television; as a senior instructor in the BBC's Television Training Department and as a lecturer at the London Institute.

In 1982 he published *On Camera*. Its three editions (1982, 1984, 1997) have became a standard text for media students and recruits to the profession. A fourth edition is now in preparation. His *On Camera* training tapes collected 6 awards in the UK, US and Australia. His second book, *Directing On Camera*, was published in 1992. *Instant On Camera* is his latest.

INSTANT ON CAMERA

Storytelling

Briefings

Drama

Briefings

INSTANT ON CAMERA

Factual Programmes

Briefings

Going Solo

On Camera books

Instant On Camera is the third of the *On Camera* books. All the books approach programme-making in a different way. The first, *On Camera*, takes you through the production process from ideas to publicity and covers all types of programme (single-camera, studio, outside broadcasts). It also offers twenty briefings on subjects as diverse as technology, sound, editing, processing and editing film, lighting and getting a job in TV.

Directing On Camera concentrates on single-camera directing and editing and discusses the implications for directors of how we perceive pictures.

Using *Instant On Camera*

You can use *Instant On Camera* as a programme-making course by working through the three stages (*Storytelling*, *Drama* and *Factual Programmes*) and doing the projects.

Or you can use *Instant On Camera* for information and advice about whichever part of the programme-making process you are tackling by consulting the relevant briefings.

However you use the book, you should take on board the key concepts and their implications for practical programme-making as discussed at the start of each section.

Going Solo covers 'self-op' - programme-making without a crew. It's worth reading, even if you never touch a camera, as it offers the basic technical grounding you need to be a good director.

Key concepts

Storytelling
- Shooting is collecting pictures and sound for editing
- Shoot the complete action, not just the bit you might use
- Shoot reaction as well as action
- Where practical, start and end people out of shot
- Keep your editing options open
- Think ahead

Drama
- Shoot for the screen
- Shoot close-ups
- Use light and shadow
- Get an angle

Factual Programmes
- Show things happening

Projects

For those using *Instant On Camera* as a programme-making course, the time and resources for the project at each stage are as follows.

The *Storytelling* project needs a little preparation, one or two actors, an hour's shoot and a couple of hours in the editing room.

The *Drama* project is a development of *Storytelling*. This time you are encouraged to concentrate on getting more effective shots, using light creatively and giving your story dramatic impact on the screen. You need a more ambitious story, two actors with possibly a walk-on or two, two to three hours' shooting and about six hours' editing.

Factual Programmes explains techniques you will need for documentary and encourages you to apply these and the techniques you acquired on the *Storytelling* and *Drama* projects to a genuine documentary subject. The scale, time and resources for this exercise are left to you, but the briefing on *Time and money* gives you a practical way of working out what these might be.

Introduction

There are two ways to make programmes. One way is based on words. You use the words as a guide and the pictures follow the words. The other way is to make the words follow the pictures.

Drama, well-made factual programmes and cinema mostly use pictures as their guide. The script is designed to put people in situations where action and reaction can be seen, not just talked about. Pictures carry most of the message; words complete the picture. When words are used as the guide, words deliver most of the message and pictures play a secondary role.

Instant On Camera puts pictures first. It focuses on the picture-driven approach to programme-making. Wherever possible, show the situation or event, rather than talk about it. Exploit the visual potential of the medium as much as you can. The concept behind this book is don't tell me, show me.

The case for picture-driven programmes is straightforward. Pictures are powerful and directly engage the emotions. Emotional experiences are the rewards that keep people viewing. They want to experience happiness, tears, laughter, suspense, fear, as well as emotions (such as desire) that aren't normally mentioned in polite company. They want to experience all this for themselves, at a safe distance and without suffering any personal consequences.

Words, of course, can also be powerful and engage the emotions. But in a visual medium where there always has to be something on screen - if only to show there hasn't been a breakdown - viewers are short-changed if the pictures are just screen-fillers. General shots of hospitals and schools to illustrate health and education stories may be unavoidable in news bulletins, but if that's all there is to separate the sound bites, you begin to wonder why you need to watch as well as listen. Television is more than radio with pictures.

Think pictures.

Storytelling

Storytelling key concepts

Shooting is collecting pictures and sound for editing

Programme-making is like cooking for a dinner party. You prepare a treatment or storyboard (decide on a menu), shoot the material (buy the ingredients), and then edit (make the meal in the kitchen). When you are shooting, you are collecting the ingredients; you're shooting for editing. The film* is not made on location. It's made in the cutting room.

Several things follow.

Shoot the complete action, not just the bit you might use

This gives you greater choice in the cutting room. If you do a close-up and a wider shot of the whole action, you can cut from close-up to wide shot or vice versa at any point. Or use just one of the shots, if it does the job alone. Covering the complete action in both shots is counter-intuitive - why shoot stuff you don't think you'll use? Beginners often forget to do it. Later in the cutting room, when planned edits don't work and other edits can't be tried because the material isn't there, they wish they had remembered.

Shooting the whole action also helps the performers. It makes it easier to avoid continuity mistakes. If actors have to keep stopping, they are more likely to forget details, like which hand they used to do something. It's also easier to perform the whole action in one go, rather than break it down into action-bites that the director thinks may edit well.

---

* I use 'film' interchangeably with 'programme' and 'shoot', even if the 'film' originated, or is being shot, on video.

Shoot reaction as well as action

You reap the same rewards if you also shoot reactions in one long take.

Most screen events can be split into concurrent events: one person talks, the other listens; one does, the other watches; one travels, the other stays at home. The duration of these events is often inconvenient for the screen. Covering the whole reaction provides cutaways that allow you to compress or lengthen events in the cutting room, so that you can milk the drama.

Where practical, start and end people out of shot

If you do a shot of a man coming out of a house, don't start the shot when the front door is half open. Start before he opens it. This gives you great freedom about which shot you put before the front-door shot. You could, for example, use a shot of the man fast asleep in bed. There's no difficulty if you cut from him in bed to a shot of the door before it opens.

But cutting from the man in bed to a shot of him already visible through the half-open door could be an awkward jump cut. If you start shooting before the door opens, you have a choice of starting points in the cutting room.

Keep your editing options open

All the points above form part of a general strategy for shooting: keep your editing options open.

This isn't an excuse for not working out a shooting style or strategy. It's a recognition that pressures while you are shooting (not enough time, changing light, deteriorating weather, noise from trains, aircraft and traffic, etc.) make locations a bad place to judge what the impact and duration of shots may be in the finished programme. And your editor will love you for providing material that he or she can do something with.

Think ahead

At each stage in making a programme you need to keep half your mind on the next stage. So when you are doing a recce, think about the shots. When you are shooting, think how the shots might cut together. When you are editing, think about the commentary and dub.

Proper preparation prevents poor performance.

Storytelling project

Objective
Cover a visual incident that can be edited for maximum impact on screen.

Shooting time
One hour. Why limit yourself to an hour? If you're on a training course, a time limit is needed to give everyone on the course a chance to shoot their own project. If you aren't on a course, it's a good discipline to learn to shoot in a business-like way, because no matter whether you're shooting for love or money, there's never enough time. At this stage making a crisp point on screen will teach you more than delivering a long drawn out fudge.

Editing time
Two hours with an experienced editor, longer if you are working the equipment yourself. You may learn a lot from editing different versions and comparing their effect on viewers or reviewers. (See *Review your work* below.)

Duration
40 to 60 seconds, but the exact duration doesn't matter. The important thing is to find the most effective duration for the material. So edit it to what it's worth.

Location
Preferably outdoors, so that you don't have to worry about lighting. Find somewhere quiet and away from road traffic.

Cast
One or two people, depending on your story.

Hints
Put your emphasis in this project on **action and reaction rather than words**. Instead of an extended dialogue, limit your actors to 10 words on screen. In one hour's **shooting time** you'll have time for about 6 shots - 20 minutes for the first (it rarely takes less time) and 6 to 7 minutes for each camera position or setup after that. If you can do more than one shot from a setup (in other words, without moving the camera to another position), allow about 2 minutes for each extra shot.

You will be better prepared to shoot this exercise if you **draw a simple storyboard** in advance (See *Planning with a storyboard and bird's-eye view* on page 24 for how to do this). Storyboards force you to think about the shots you will need and help you avoid the most obvious mistakes. Plan not more than 7 shots. You won't be able to shoot more in 60 minutes.

You need to be realistic when planning your story but be ambitious as well. **Don't just play safe.** Try an approach or a shot that goes a little beyond what you know you can pull off. The beauty of a training exercise is that it doesn't have to work. Don't be frightened of mistakes — you learn by them.

What makes a good story? Something that engages the emotions. If you think about it, the programmes and films that you enjoy are the ones that make you laugh or cry or excite or thrill or intrigue or surprise you.

The desire to tell people about a programme is also a useful test. If you see a good programme, you are likely to tell your friends about it the next day. If it's bad, you probably won't mention it. Unless it's so bad that it invites contempt or ridicule. There are Turkey awards as well as Oscars.

Finally, **take your programme-making seriously**, but have fun. Making a programme is hard work but if you don't enjoy making it, what chance have the viewers?

Story suggestion: The greeting

Two people meet and greet each other. Give the incident your own twist. Remember, no more than 10 words.

Story suggestion: The message

Someone receives a message by mobile phone or letter or fax, or a notice pinned on a tree or stuck to a car windscreen, or any other means you choose. Is the news good or bad? What does he or she do?

Depending on the story, you may need more than one actor. Remember to draw or write the message in advance; remember also to take with you envelopes, drawing pins or sticky tape as required. If the actor has to crumple or tear up the message, you will need several copies.

Story suggestion: Banana skin

Slipping on a banana skin is a cliché gag (like walking under a ladder or trousers falling down) that can be given an un-expected twist. The challenge is to find the shots that set up an expectation in the viewer that may - or may not - be fulfilled.

The director's role

Take control

Why have a director? The cameraman* has almost certainly shot more films than the director. Why not let him or her do the job?

The cameraman could indeed do so, but is unlikely to do anything more than cover the action in the most straightforward way. This is because the day of the shoot is probably his only involvement in the project. He wasn't there for the planning, doesn't know what material exists or is planned, or how it will be edited. Introducing a personal style or shooting from unusual angles could make his material difficult to fit in with the rest. So most cameramen very sensibly play safe.

The director is in a different position. He or she sees the project through from beginning to end. It's his film.

So your first function as a director on location is to take control. Like the conductor of an orchestra you're there to set the approach, tone and pace of the proceedings.

This doesn't mean that you act as a dictator, laying down the law on everything. Listen to what the crew say and adopt their suggestions, if they fit in with your ideas. But remember that there can be too many suggestions, particularly when you are unsure how to proceed. Don't waste time considering all of them. Decide as soon as you can which way you, the director, want to do it. If you can't decide, choose a couple of ways of proceeding, shoot them both and decide which works best in the cutting room.

The tone you set on location is also important. If you are well-prepared, good-humoured and business-like, your crew and performers will knock themselves out to help you. If you aren't, people will be less helpful. Why should they knock themselves out for your film, if you can't be bothered to do so yourself?

Setting the pace is another part of your job. The black hole between finishing one shot and setting up the next eats up time. Once you have said 'Cut' and checked that everyone is happy, move straight on to the next shot. Don't dither around. Keep things moving and everyone will be happier. At the end of the day they will all feel they have done a good day's work and not wasted their time. And think of you as a good director.

'Cameraman' includes women who do the job. It's the best word to use because it emphasises the job (important), rather than the gender of the person who does it (unimportant).

Starting and stopping

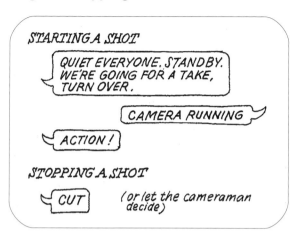

The commands for starting and stopping are great for focusing everybody's mind on the shot. Obviously if everyone is already quiet and standing by, you don't need to say 'Quiet' and 'Standby'. You also don't need to say 'Action' in all situations. In intimate scenes or scenes with children or animals, a loud 'Action' cuts right across the mood you are trying to create. A quiet 'Ready when you are' or 'In your own time' or a simple hand gesture is more sensitive and effective.

In the same way, you don't really need to say 'Cut' unless there are a lot of performers. Tell the cameraman in advance you aren't going to say 'Cut' and then let him or her decide when the shot is over. If you do say 'Cut', wait a couple of beats after the action is over before you make the announcement. The editing rhythm may need the extra bit of shot.

When a shot is completed to your satisfaction, check that the performers and crew are happy. If they are, move on to the next shot without delay.

Try always to be positive with the performers. The camera gives no feedback and makes everyone - even professionals - feel vulnerable, so a word of approval is always welcome. Besides, if you say nothing, the performers may decide to do something different for the retake.

See also *Working with actors* on page 67.

Learn the names of the shot sizes

Use the right language as much as possible. It's clearer and faster, makes you sound professional and gives confidence to your colleagues that you're on top of the job. Use the names of shot sizes below to indicate what you want. Or use your arms to show the edges of the shot you have in mind.

LS - Long Shot
MLS - Medium Long Shot
MS - Mid-shot

MCU - Medium Close-up
CU - Close-up
BCU - Big Close-up

Differentiate the camera moves

The most important words are pan, zoom, tilt and move. You must get them right to sound professional when talking to anyone in the business. Note that the camera stays in the same place for the pan, zoom and tilt. If it moves over the ground, you can say track or dolly or - easiest of all - move.

Camera right and left

When you are on location or in the studio, it's normal practice always to refer to right and left from the camera's point of view. Use the terms 'camera right' or 'camera left'.

This gets round the confusion arising from the fact that right and left are on different sides, depending on whether you're facing the camera or behind it.

It also helps to back up what you say by pointing.

CAMERA RIGHT   CAMERA LEFT

Today, briefly

At the start of a shoot (always get to the location early), everyone needs an outline of what is planned to happen. Explain the story or action for the day in three or four sentences, not more.

Such brevity may not come naturally, so practise before the shoot. Brevity has many benefits. It lets everyone know what is happening. It signals that you know what you are doing. And it forces you to collect your thoughts. Often if you have been working on a project for some time, your mind is so full of ideas and possibilities that you aren't really sure where you're going. Working on a summary concentrates the mind.

If you are undecided about an aspect of the story, say so. Plans don't have to be rigid.

Rehearse the whole sequence

When you have set the shape for the day, you need to make sure there is something coherent to shoot. Rehearse the whole sequence with your performers before worrying about camera positions and shots. This may sound odd advice, but novice directors are often so worried about the shots that they forget about the action. If the action isn't right or the performers don't know what they are doing, it's difficult to act convincingly. So rehearse your performers first, then worry about the camera.

When you rehearse you will find that there are some areas of uncertainty that need to be cleared up: for example, how exactly is character A going to show the map to character B? Which hand will it be in? How will A and B stand in relation to each other? While this rehearsing is going on, your crew will be watching and may have thoughts about shots and camera positions. If you're lucky, these may be more interesting than the ones you have in mind.

Watch from the camera's point of view

When the action is beginning to work, start watching it from the camera's point of view. Then position the camera and do a final rehearsal for camera and sound. Stand behind the camera for this final rehearsal or watch the scene on the monitor and listen on headphones.

Is the camera in the best place to see the action? If it isn't, why not?

How not to communicate

If you brief people well, they can help you. If you use the approaches listed here, they won't want to. *Crew reaction in italics - unspoken, if you are lucky.* (My comments in brackets.)

You: 'I'm not very good at this. I'm not sure my idea will work.' *In that case, let's stop wasting our time and go home.* (Don't put yourself down.)

You: 'I haven't had time to think about this or prepare.' *Why not?* (If you really haven't, at least have the sense to keep quiet.)

You: 'Sorry I'm late. There's a lot to do, so we'll have to work even harder.' *Why are you late? We were here on time. Why don't you work harder?* (Don't be late. Always be early.)

You: 'I want to start on a tight close-up as she comes out of the door. Hmm, er... or perhaps a wider shot might be better. What do you think?' *I haven't a clue. You haven't told us what the film is about.* (First things first.)

You: 'Pan straight into his eyes.' *Does he mean zoom or move the camera forward?* (Use the right language.)

You: 'The sound isn't important.' *Great, we can all have our mobiles on.* (Always record sound.)

You: 'This film is all about mood, about delicate changes to sensibilities that we can't see.' *Then why are we making a film about it?* (Think pictures.)

You: 'Oh, you're shooting with the Mark 2. The resolution/ sensitivity ratio isn't as good as on the Mark 4.' *Pratt!* (Don't bullshit.)

You: 'This film has gotta be bigger than Bond.' *Then why doesn't it have a budget to match? And why are you directing it?* (Don't get carried away. Keep you feet on the ground.)

You: 'Of course, I'm used to working on 35 mm with a full crew.' *(Unprintable.)* (There are better ways of getting the crew on your side.)

You: 'I take my inspiration from Bergman.' *Bully for you. How will that help this piece to camera?* (It's also not the best moment to mention your fluent Swedish.)

Planning with a storyboard and bird's-eye view

The advantage of planning is that it lets you make your mistakes on paper, where they don't matter. It helps you to avoid the obvious pitfalls and find better ways of shooting, even before you set foot on location.

Some people worry that planning cramps improvisation and creativity. Not true. It fosters them. It doesn't have to be rigid. If you get a better idea when you're shooting, there is no reason why you shouldn't adopt it.

If anything, planning helps you to get lucky on the shoot.

Don't think that storyboards and such-like are for beginners and wimps only. Major Hollywood movie-makers do storyboards and the results are sometimes published. You could do worse than look through one or two in a bookshop or library.

You can plan either with pictures (storyboard or bird's-eye view) or by writing a treatment. This section is about planning with pictures. *Planning with a treatment* is on page 94.

Storyboard

A storyboard is basically a cartoon strip. Draw a picture for each shot that you intend to take. If it's a complicated shot, draw two pictures. Label each picture with a shot size or camera move (if any) and a couple of words describing the shot or dialogue.

Can't draw? Use pin men or sausage men. Storyboards are a planning tool; they don't have to be works of art.

Doing a storyboard is hard work, but rewarding. All sorts of knotty shooting and directing problems will come to mind as you do it - conveniently, while you have the time and energy to think about the best way round them.

You'll find that you keep on going back and changing ideas you had for covering a particular action.

Good. You've really started to think.

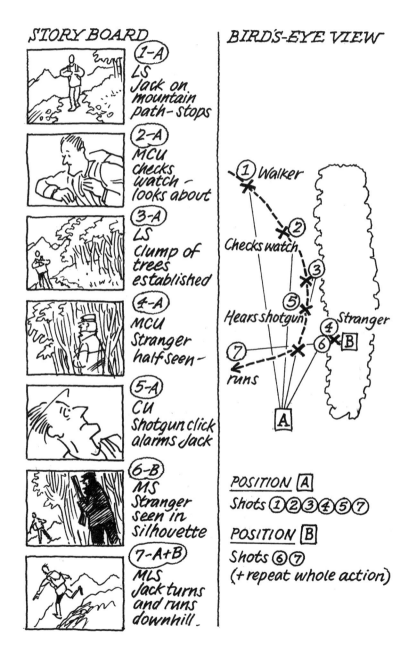

STORY BOARD

1-A
LS
Jack on
mountain
path-stops

2-A
MCU
checks
watch -
looks about

3-A
LS
clump of
trees
established

4-A
MCU
Stranger
half seen -

5-A
CU
Shotgun click
alarms Jack

6-B
MS
Stranger
seen in
silhouette

7-A+B
MLS
Jack turns
and runs
downhill.

BIRD'S-EYE VIEW

① Walker

② Checks watch

③

⑤
Hears shotgun

④ Stranger
⑥ B
⑦
runs

A

POSITION A
Shots ①②③④⑤⑦

POSITION B
Shots ⑥⑦
(+ repeat whole action)

Using a storyboard

When you've finished your storyboard, analyse the results. Are there too many long shots? Are there enough close-ups? Are too many of the shots the same size? Can you introduce more variety? Can you make more of the dramatic highlights? Can you change the camera position or the position of the performers to produce a more effective shot?

How many shots have you planned? Do you have any chance of shooting them in the time available? Use your storyboard to find the answer.

Allow at least 20 minutes for doing the first shot. It will take all of that to unpack the gear, plug in all the bits, organise everyone to be in the right positions and turn over the camera. After the first shot you can assume that it will take 6 or 7 minutes for each camera position; add a couple of minutes for each extra shot from the same position. If you have to light or change the lights for a shot, allow 10 minutes per shot.

Tot up the minutes. If the total is more than the time available, put a mark beside the shots that are vital. If the total for must-have shots is still over the top, you need a serious rethink.

Bird's-eye view

It's also helpful to do a bird's-eye view of each location. Show the main features that will affect the camera positions: for exteriors: houses, cars, trees, bushes etc.; for interiors: furniture, doors and windows. Then put in the camera positions you have in mind.

Will the camera be able to see the things you expect from these positions? Are you crossing the line? (See next page.)

On the shoot

When you meet your performers and crew, let them see that you have done a storyboard and bird's eye view but don't spend time talking them through it. Give them instead a brief summary of the story and the plan for the day (see *Today, briefly* on page 22). They will be impressed by the care with which you prepared and your ability to tell them what they need to know in a few sentences. They'll be more willing to help you because you have done your homework.

Good planning gets the crew and performers on your side.

Crossing the line

You are filming someone running through the park. If you put the camera on one side of the path, the man is running left to right. With the camera on the other side, he will be running right to left.

Camera anywhere this side of the line shows runner moving right.

Camera anywhere this side of the line shows runner moving left.

Camera on the line shows runner approaching.

If you are taking a lot of shots and want to cross over for some reason, take shots from the middle of the path of the man coming towards or going away from the camera. As far as continuity of direction is concerned, these shots are neutral. The next shot can then show the man moving across the screen in either direction.

If you take shots from both sides of the path and intercut the results, the changes in direction on screen will be quite violent.

For viewers the changes in direction can be confusing, as the background may also change. Perhaps there are fields on one side and houses on the other. On screen the viewer might think the man has turned round and is in a different location.

If you want to take shots of two people walking down the path talking to each other, you can shoot from the front or from behind - no problem. But if you want to see them from each other's point of view you have to shoot from both sides of the path.

Background moves left   Background moves right

When you cut these shots together the two people will be looking in the right directions (screen right and screen left) but the background will appear to be moving in different directions. This is because there are two lines in this situation: the line joining the talkers and the line of their movement down the path. You can't help crossing one of these lines.

Multiple lines

Things become even more complicated in dinner parties and courtroom scenes, where there are people at all points of the compass and the line changes for each person.

In such situations it's best to do a master shot to cover the whole action. Then shoot close-ups and two-shots and so on.

Also shoot a range of reaction shots: people looking right and left and turning from one side to another and back again. For good measure, do a 'get out of jail free' shot as well: the cat curled up on the sofa, or a shot from the next room through an open door or through a window. The editor should then have enough material to sort out any problems that may crop up.

If in doubt

There may be times when you aren't sure where the line is, or you and the cameraman see it in a different way. When this happens, don't waste time talking about it. Shoot it both ways. Then decide which way looks best in the edit suite.

One final bit of advice. Don't worry about crossing the line. It's not as taboo as it used to be.

Safety

Don't skip this section. As director you - yes, you - are one of the people responsible for the safety of the performers and crew during the shoot. You could end up in court if you ignore safety requirements.

You may be a normal, sensible person in ordinary life. But the excitement and pressure of film-making can do strange things to your judgement. Don't get so engrossed in the film that you forget to use your common sense.

Here are some of the obvious things to think about. For anything more out of the ordinary you need expert help. If you are worried about the cost of expert help, remember it works out a lot cheaper than the court case, both financially and in terms of your career. More importantly, something priceless - like life or health - may be involved.

First aid
Go on a course and always take a first-aid kit with you.

Traffic
Just because a road is quiet doesn't mean it isn't used. So think about what happens if a car appears. Will you be able to see it in time? Will it be able to see you in time? Will it be travelling fast? Will you be able to get out of the way?

At the very least you must position a lookout to warn you of approaching traffic - or two lookouts, if you are exposed in both directions. If the actors or crew have to stand in the road for any length of time, you need more elaborate precautions - police permission, cones, warning signs and high visibility jackets. It's better to find a private road that the owner doesn't mind you blocking off completely.

Roadsides
Narrow pavements are a problem because you may be forcing passers-by to step into the road. You have no right to make them do this. Narrow pavements also make it all too easy for one of your team concentrating on a technical or acting problem to step into the road during a lull in the traffic. What happens when the next batch of speeding traffic arrives?

Setting up an accident

Here's how. You ask a driver to stop 'here'. 'Right here,' you say, pointing to the spot. You then place the camera on the stopping point. He drives up, stopping as directed. And runs down the camera. 'I thought the cameraman was going to yank it away at the last moment,' the driver says.

The accident is your fault. Whenever you fix a stopping place, mark it with an out-of-shot pair of cones or some other marker. Make sure the driver knows what you are using for markers and understands what you want him to do. Then position the camera at least three metres back from the marker. Or you're asking for trouble.

Even with this precaution there may be problems. There could be a misunderstanding. Or the driver forgets what he agreed. Or the agreed markers aren't as visible from the driving seat as you both thought. Or the driver wants to give you an exciting shot, drives faster than usual and can't stop in time. Or he skids. Does the cameraman need to be behind the camera? Can't he start the camera and watch from the sidelines?

The way to make things look more exciting on screen than they are in real life is to take a low shot or make the shot tighter. And then speed up the shot in the edit suite.

Actors

Actors often fib about how well they can drive, or ride horses, or fence, or even ride a bicycle. They want the job.

Exaggerating driving ability is particularly dangerous. If you have any doubts, ask the actor to drive round a car park before you start filming. If any doubt remains about the actor's driving experience or ability, use another driver and shoot the car in such a way that the driver isn't visible.

This basic precaution is sufficient only for normal driving in a standard private car. Anything larger (lorries or vans), faster (sports cars) or less common (motor-bikes or scooters) needs a specialist driver.

If you are thinking of doing skids or faking crashes or anything at speed - don't. The excitement you want on screen can be generated very effectively by a bit of imagination and noises off (you show the car driving out of shot; later you dub on a screech of tyres, a crash, the car radio still playing etc.) Anything more visible and you need a professional stunt man - as you do if you want to stage sword fights or fisticuffs.

Stunt men are always cheaper than the court case.

Trips and falls

Provide a mattress or cushions to break falls on hard surfaces. Put the camera low on the ground and shoot upwards so that the break-falls can't be seen. On soft or mucky surfaces provide a blanket or rug to protect actors' clothing.

Flying

If you are hiring a plane or hitching a ride on a helicopter, start planning early. There are details about licences and insurance that you need to sort out before take-off. You may find that some tempting options, like paying for a cameraman to go up in a hang glider or microlight, are illegal in the UK.

If you fly with a helicopter door open to give the cameraman more scope, make sure everyone (not just the cameraman) is strapped in and everything (camera cases, cassettes, bags, brief cases, mobile phones etc.) is secured. Anything left loose in the cabin is liable to exit through the open door. If it hits anyone on the ground, the loss of a piece of equipment will be the least of your problems.

Power lines

Electricity cables are obviously dangerous for aircraft. They can also be dangerous if you're on the ground.

You don't have to make contact with a cable to get a lethal shock; if you get too close, the current can arc or flash to your equipment. The gun mic on a pole is particularly at risk.

Also, don't assume that cables slung from wooden poles are telephone wires. They could be power lines.

Riots

A riot may give you great pictures but is it worth risking your life to get them? You feel braver behind a camera but you are also more conspicuous and vulnerable. Will your camera equipment, press badge or station logo (is there one on the car?) offer you protection or make you a target? Are you encouraging more violence by filming it? Tough questions, but you need to face them.

Working alone

If you are going solo, you need to take extra precautions. There's more about this in *Safety and security* on page 158.

Risk assessment and insurance

Your company may require you to fill out a risk assessment form. This forces you to think about what you intend to do, identify the hazards and quantify the risks. Failure to comply with this procedure may invalidate the company's insurance policy. If you are an independent, do your own risk assessment and insure yourself for at least public liability.

Safety websites

The BBC's safety rules and guidance are available free for anyone to consult on *www.bbc-safety.co.uk*. The approach is positive and there's a wealth of fascinating detail. There's also an A to Z Index. Definitely worth a visit.

Another website with helpful advice about health and safety is *www.shootingpeople.org*. The safety section is one of a series of Essential Guides, written especially for programme-makers. These provide information on a range of useful topics, some of them unexpected- like finding and contracting actors or finding a distributor for your film, topics that it's difficult to find help on elsewhere.

Editing basics

(Use this section in conjunction with *Editing drama* on page 76 and *Editing factual programmes* on page 103.)

Editing is cutting pictures and sound together to achieve the maximum impact on screen. It's the process of choosing the best shots and the best part of each shot and putting them in the best order to tell the story. When it's done well, the final cut adds up to more than the sum of the shots. You get a buzz of satisfaction and want to show the result to friends and colleagues.

When you are editing, stay in the cutting room and work with the editor. It's the best place to learn to direct, second only to actually directing. You see the shots that work and the ones that don't. You also see which shots are missing.

Preparation

Tell the editor what the story is about and then view the material together while it is being loaded into the editing machine. This process is known as digitising or capturing and usually has to be done in real time, so it can take an hour or more, depending on how much material there is.

You can speed up the process by making a VHS copy with burnt-in time code and seeing if there is any material you definitely won't want to use. Don't be too selective at this stage. Just identify chunks that you won't need to digitise.

First assembly

1   Do a first assembly by putting the shots and their accompanying sound roughly in the right order. Top and tail the shots, but don't worry about the cuts at this stage.

2   View this first assembly. You should be able to see a rough outline of your story.

3   Some shots (or parts of shots) may show the same action twice.
Each shot should move the action on or add something to the story. (*If it doesn't, drop it.*)

Fine cut

1   Now trim the beginnings and ends of shots to make the cuts work.

Cut on action. *(Action cuts make smooth cuts. Cuts between static objects tend to jar.)*

Don't cut between same size shots of the same subject. *(Cuts between different size shots work better.)*

Don't cut unless you have to. *(Keep a shot on screen as long as it's working - no longer. Don't cut to another shot of the same thing just because you have one.)*

Shorter is better. *(If in doubt, cut it out.)*

2   View the story again. It should now be close to its final shape. Some parts of the story will be weaker than others. For these parts ask yourself:

Is there a better shot we can use? *(It can be worth looking through the original material again, because you will now know what you are looking for.)*

Would changing the order of shots help? *(If changing the order doesn't help and you can't find a better shot, drop the weak section.)*

Finally

1   Show the story to someone else, preferably someone with programme-making experience (see *Review your work* on page 37). The other person comes fresh to your story, so he or she may see it in a different way. If there is a difference of opinion, the other person is almost certainly right.

2   When you have finished editing, the machine may have to reassemble the story so that it can be recorded onto tape, a process known as conforming or rendering. This is necessary because nonlinear editing machines never actually assemble the programme. Instead they keep an edit decision list - the EDL. Playback is provided by instantly retrieving the shots on the EDL from the computer memory.

3   If you have been editing on an offline setup (below broadcast quality) you may have to take the EDL to an online setup (broadcast quality) where the programme will be assembled from the original recordings.

Going solo - instant introduction

Going solo - operating the camera and directing at the same time - is not the easy option for programme-makers. The following are merely guidelines. For more detailed help see the *Going Solo* section after page 126.

1   First of all you have to know how to operate the camera really well. Practise until it's second nature. You should be able to cope with most problems of focus, aperture and recording without looking at the controls or referring to the manual.

2   The same is true for sound. This will be more complicated to master, but persevere. Viewers will tolerate poor pictures. If the sound is poor, they will switch off.

3   Manual or auto? In straightforward situations the auto systems work fine. But there are many situations where they don't work so well. So you have to know when and how to switch to manual. (See the *Explore* sections in *Going Solo*.)

4   The way to make a success of solo operating, directing and interviewing is to prepare well. Research, recce, treatment or storyboard, topics for interviews and so on - the better you prepare, the better your results.

5   When you're solo, it's tempting to handhold the camera at all times. But in some situations (speeches, sit-down interviews) you really do need a tripod. In other situations a monopod with a shoulder strap may be sufficient. Always take the tripod or monopod with you, in case you need it.

6   Try to resist endless panning and zooming while shooting. The zoom control may make you feel in charge, but nonstop use doesn't mean you are composing an interesting shot.

7   When you are familiar with camera and sound, think about editing. How do you transfer your recorded shots to the editing equipment? How many sound tracks can the equipment handle? What about stereo? What about time code?

8   Don't try to edit while you're shooting. Shoot to edit.

9   Going solo is more dangerous than working with a crew, for both you and your equipment. You need to follow different routines and procedures to reduce the risks.

10   Is the project you're doing suitable for going solo? See *Safety* on page 30 and *Safety and security* on page 158.

Review your work

The judge and jury of your film are, of course, the viewers. By the time they see it, however, it's too late to make changes. Arranging a test screening can be helpful, but it's rarely possible.

There is also a problem with previewing work to people who aren't programme-makers. They tend to see films as givens, while programme-makers know that films are the result of choices. So viewers can rarely tell you why something did or didn't work.

A programme-maker, on the other hand, may be able to analyse the problem and suggest a remedy: one less shot here, a change in shot order there, or why not add a shot to make something work better (a shot you usually don't have)?

Try and find someone who is encouraging and recognises the constraints of time, equipment and budget you faced while making your programme. Someone who is willing to review the programme you have actually made, not the one he or she would have made. Criticism for criticism's sake or destructive criticism that emphasises your reviewer's superior knowledge, ability and access to resources are not helpful.

On the other hand, don't be too thin-skinned about accepting criticism. If you can't take some flak, you are in the wrong business.

The time to call in a programme-maker to review your film is somewhere between the rough-cut and the fine cut, when you can still change things and thus take advantage of his or her comments - if you want to. You can, after all, agree to differ. Sometimes it may be the right thing to do.

Finally, when you show your film to a reviewer or viewers, don't introduce it with long explanations, excuses for the shots you missed, disclaimers for weak points and (worst of all) comments about the shortcomings of the performers and crew. These signal a lack of confidence in your product and make you look weak.

Let the film speak for itself and let people make up their own minds. They might even like it!

Drama

Drama key concepts

Shoot for the screen

In *Storytelling* the emphasis was on recording the pictures and sound needed to make a story in the edit. For this stage you should work on a drama - even if your main interest is factual programming - and concentrate on the photographic quality of the shots. Are they well composed? Are they well lit? Are they interesting? Will they work on screen?

In other words, shoot for the screen.

Shoot close-ups

Close-ups are a strength of television. They have impact, show viewers what you want them to see and exclude what you don't want them to see.

Our eyes and brain working together automatically go to the closest possible view, even if we are standing metres away from what we are looking at. The camera can't do this automatically. You have to move it closer to the object, or zoom in. (Note that these actions produce different sorts of close-ups, because they change the depth of field and the relative distance between objects in different ways. See *Lenses* on page 58.)

Use light and shadow

Light is eye-catching, shadow is dramatic. You don't always need expensive lighting to get beautiful shots. A small change to the light you find on (or bring to) the location can often make a big difference. You can turn ordinary shots into interesting ones by changing the way light falls on the subject or background.

1   Close or open a curtain or shutter or door.

2   Add a reflector to soften the shadows.

3   Can you improve the shot by changing the distance and/or angle between subject and light?

4   Shoot against the light.

5   If there are several lamps on the subject, try switching one or two off to see the effect.

(See *Light* on page 52.)

Get an angle

Shooting from the front with the camera at the subject's eye height is the most straightforward covering shot. Sometimes it's the right shot.

But you can often find a more effective shot by changing the position or height of the camera. (See *Looking for good shots* on page 47 and *Composition* on page 50.)

Drama project

Objective
Shoot and edit a short story with visual impact.

Shooting time
2½ to 3 hours.

Editing time
5 to 6 hours with an experienced editor, longer if you are working the equipment yourself.

Duration
Anything between 2½ and 4 minutes, but as with the *Storytelling* project, the duration isn't important. Don't worry about it. Concentrate on making the story as effective as possible on screen.

Location
Indoors or outdoors, but choose locations close to each other and to base. If you don't, you will spend too much time moving between locations, and not enough time shooting.

Cast
2 people. Possibly 1 or 2 extras.

Storyboard
Do a storyboard as explained in *Planning with a storyboard and bird's-eye view* on page 24. Then check each shot in the storyboard to make sure that you are shooting for the screen. Have you included close-ups, used light and shadow and thought about camera angles?

Use the storyboard to sort out costumes before the shoot. You will have to provide any special items, but if the performers can wear their normal clothes, contact them a day or two before the shoot to brief them on your preferences: formal or casual, coats, sunglasses, hats etc. Confirm what you have agreed by email, if possible.

You should also make a written list of the props that you will need. Who is going to acquire them and look after them during the shoot? Who is going to return them after the shoot?

Estimating shooting time

Use the storyboard to estimate your shooting time.

1   Allow time to brief and rehearse the performers (assuming that you aren't able to organise a rehearsal before the shooting day - highly recommended).

2   Allow time to brief the crew.

3   Allow at least 20 minutes for unpacking the equipment, setting up and shooting the first shot.

4   Allow 6-7 minutes for each setup, longer if you are using extra lights.

5   Allow time both to pack up the equipment and to tidy up the location after the shoot. Leave the location as you found it.

6   If these calculations show you won't have enough time to shoot the story, highlight the shots you must have and give them priority. That way you know you have the story.

Using time well

1   You are always short of time on location. But don't get too carried away by the need for haste. If a shot hasn't worked after two takes, it's probably not a good idea to abandon it because you're behind schedule. Invest the time needed to get the shot right. In the end viewers see the shots, not the schedule.

2   As far as possible, shoot scenes in the order they appear in the story. It's easier for actors, make-up and continuity.

3   Make an exception to shooting in the order of the story if it means that you have to go back to a location. Whenever possible, shoot all the scenes on one location before moving to the next. This can be difficult if the characters in your film develop and it begins and ends on the same location.

4   Some shots will take less than 6-7 minutes to shoot, some more. Don't spend a disproportionate amount of time on shots that will be on screen only briefly.

5   If you leave the final scene to the end, make sure you allow enough time to do it well. The final scene is probably the most important scene in the film. Don't give it the poorest coverage. If necessary, simplify coverage of other scenes so that you know you have time to do it justice.

Drama story suggestions

For this project you need a more ambitious story than the one you shot for *Storytelling*. You are no longer rationed to 10 words but try and devise a story that isn't just two people talking. Try to show things happening. A happening doesn't have to be violent or large-scale. A look, a hesitation, a raised eyebrow, revelation, confrontation or emotion are all things happening.

The chase

Someone realises they are being followed. They try to get away. What happens when the pursuer catches up? Or doesn't? For an exciting chase on screen you need to invent 'business', such as pursuer or pursued tripping up, knocking over dustbins, leaping over obstacles, and coming to doors that won't open. Remember that runners get out of breath. Actors get their breath back between shots and forget to pant again for the next shot. They should look increasingly breathless as the chase develops.

An awkward situation

Someone is working late in the office, alone. A colleague appears, drunk and threatening. What happens? This story gives opportunities for trying out some interesting lighting.

Sandwich (sandwish) lunch

Someone eating a sandwich lunch in the park sees a person he or she fantasises about. Use a style (like overexposing) for the 'dream' shots.

Mobile encounter

Mobile phones (and text and voice messages) offer a wealth of dramatic possibilities. The caller or called may be in difficulties, or being stalked or overheard.

Ghost story

A mobile rings after a funeral. It's a call from the deceased… Use locked-off shots to make ghosts appear and vanish. See page 92 for how to do a locked-off shot.

Surreptitious smoker

With smoking banned in most shared spaces, what lengths do addicts have to go to for their fix?

Silent movie

Expressive acting with lots of gestures can be a fun way to tell a story.

How we look at shots

If you want eye-catching shots you have to know what catches the eye. Even on small screens, eyes fix on points of interest in the picture rather than on the picture as a whole. The points of interest that catch the eye are usually movement (which is why people draw attention to themselves by waving); and light (which is why theatres put the spotlight on the star).

If you want viewers to look at something that's static or in the shade, you have a problem. You may be able to steer viewers away from eye-catching movement and light by holding the shot on screen longer and using a word in the commentary to steer viewers to the target. But basically these are sticking plasters. You need to rethink the shot.

In real life your eyes and brain heavily edit what you see, even when you look at yourself in a mirror.

Your eyes and brain do far less editing for still and moving pictures. This is why seeing yourself in a picture is often a bit of a shock: 'Gosh, look at that. I look horrible. That's not what I look like.' Sorry, it is what you look like, but without the benefit of the mental airbrush.

How your eyes process a scene depends on a range of factors: gender (men and women look at each other in different ways), age (policemen aren't younger - you're older), interests (railway anoraks see details where we see a train), education (art historians see an -ism where others see paintings), profession (cameramen see light, others take it for granted) and so on.

Some useful points follow from the way our eyes work:

1   Eyes look at points of interest in the picture. If you want a smooth edit between two shots, make sure the points are in the same part of the screen. This technique also makes jump cuts work: shot A (woman walking down street) cuts smoothly with shot B (woman at door) because viewers' eyes don't have to flick to another part of the screen as the shot changes.

2   Eyes go to movement and light. Make sure the main subject in your picture is moving or in the light.

3   Or have your main subject move into the light. This triggers both eye-catching elements and adds a touch of drama.

4   Or keep the subject still and move the light to reveal the subject. See the picture on page 145.

5   What we expect to see can determine what we see. As producer/director you can't help being influenced by the work you did planning and recording the shot. So if you and the editor disagree about what a shot is saying, the editor is usually right. Your eyes have lost their innocence. The editor's eyes, however, are relatively uncompromised.

6   Surely the editor's eyes, not having been involved in planning and shooting, are completely uncompromised? Well, no. The reason is that, as the edit progresses, the editor and you get ever closer to the material. It becomes increasingly difficult to see the pictures as first-time viewers will see them. Try and make allowances for this effect. Perhaps show the film to someone who hasn't seen it before.

7   One definition of directing is to make viewers see what you see. This doesn't happen automatically. You have to make it happen.

Looking for good shots

General

1   Shoot in eye-catching places. Look for good locations, and good shots in them.

2   Work hard on the GVs (general views) as well as the crucial close-ups. Whatever their size, all shots are important.

3   In general, movement towards the camera is stronger than movement away from it. So shoot performers coming, rather than going. This lets viewers see their faces and - in the background - who or what they are walking away from.

4   Think round the action. Mirrors, reflections, shadows, shots through windows or leaves or doorways may deliver the effect you are looking for.

5   Look at the available light. What's the best way of using it for your shooting? Are there any easy ways of enhancing its photographic potential?

6   Avoid 'wallpaper'. Wallpaper shots are screen-fillers that don't contribute to the story or move it forward. They are better than a blank screen and are sometimes unavoidable for non-visual stories. But too much wallpaper turns your programme into radio with pictures.

7   Remember that cameramen - being human - don't like bending or stretching unless they have to. So they tend to keep the camera where it's most comfortable - at their own height. This isn't necessarily the ideal height for the subject. Would a higher or lower shot work better?

8   If you show you are interested in well-composed shots (as opposed to any old shot that covers the action), your camera-man will start looking for interesting shots and enjoying himself. Cameramen prefer quality to run-of-the-mill and so should you.

9   Try to avoid thinking of some shots as important and some as not so important. When you are working on a shot, treat it as the most important shot in the film.

Static shots

You want to take a shot of a person falling asleep on a park bench. Where do you put the camera? Which shot size do you use?

The **standard cover shot** - square-on from the front with the lens at the subject's (not the cameraman's) eye height.

Move the camera **higher**? Or **lower**? Will it make the shot more interesting?

Closer or **further away**? Various ways of doing this:

• Zoom in a little. Go for the essential. Show only the crucial part of the body. Do viewers need to see more?

• Instead of zooming in, move the camera closer. This increases the apparent distance between foreground and background.

• Or move the camera back and then zoom in. This makes the distance between foreground and background appear smaller (foreshortens the shot). See the pictures on page 58.

POV (point of view) shots Most shots are outside looking in. POV shots are inside looking out. The camera records the subject falling asleep from the POV of a passer-by. Or from the POV of a would-be pickpocket?

What about a **profile shot**? A shot taken from the side can offer a fresh and interesting way of looking at the subject, particularly if the light is unexpected.

The **closing frame shot**. Instead of framing the shot for the start of the action, you compose it with the end of the shot in mind. So as your subject dozes off, he slumps or falls into the picture.

Moving shots

Moving shots are more difficult to do than static shots. You need a good eye, a steady hand and possibly some special equipment like a dolly or crane or handheld stabiliser or steadicam. But don't be put off: moving shots are an essential part of the film-maker's repertoire. When done well, they draw attention to the action, not themselves.

Moving shots suffer from two particular problems. They can be difficult to cut into or out of. And it's difficult to forecast which speed for the move will look best in the edit. If in doubt, record moving shots two or more times at different speeds.

Zoom in Zooming in can emphasise detail but rarely reveals anything new. Cutting to a close-up of the detail usually does the job better.

Zoom out Zooming out is generally stronger, as the zoom reveals new information. Try and disguise zooms by making them coincide with some action in the scene.

Tracking When tracking, the camera moves over the ground; when zooming, it stays put. Tracking shots are more elegant than zooms but take more time, trouble and equipment to achieve. The cameraman can walk; or sit in a wheelchair or on a trolley, or on a special dolly on rails.

Tilt up or down Can be effective.

Motivated pan Camera follows the action to see where it's going, or what happens.

Camera moves to discover subject The camera starts on some scene-setting detail (for example, trees) and pans or tilts to arrive at the subject.

Composition

1   Allow looking room and walking room.

2   Don't leave too much room over heads (head room). Eyes should be about a third of the way down from the top of the picture.

3   The view we see most often is from normal eye height, standing or sitting. On camera it's therefore the most neutral - and probably the least interesting.

If the action is interesting, it may be the right shot. If the action is everyday (someone walking down a road, for example), will the shot be more interesting if the camera is at ground level, looking down from a first floor window, or dividing the proportion of screen occupied by person and background in an unusual way?

4   Avoid flabby shots. Fill the screen with your subject or action. Every time you line up a shot, zoom in a little further to see if tighter framing will increase its impact. But don't forget that viewers at home won't see the edges of the picture that you can see in the viewfinder (some helpful cameras can show 'picture-safe' and 'title-safe' areas in the viewfinder). The strip that viewers lose, known as cut-off, may be 2-3 cms wide on a home screen.

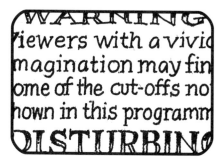

5   The screen is two-dimensional; reality is 3D. To give pictures depth:

• Change camera position so that there is something in the foreground. Or introduce something like a bicycle or a bit of foliage into the foreground (known as dingle).

• Angle shots. Don't, for example, have people standing in a line square-on to the camera; or two people on each side of the frame with a huge, empty gap between them. If this happens in the studio, you can fill the gap with something visual, but don't use a moving picture or graphic that upstages the speakers.

• Avoid even lighting. It makes pictures flat. Create shadows to give depth.

6   Sometimes reducing apparent depth can increase dramatic impact. If two people are arguing or you are doing a confrontational interview, move the camera further away and zoom in to a two-shot. The foreshortening effect makes them appear almost on top of each other, slugging it out face to face.

7   Composition is subjective. So ignoring the points above may be the right thing to do.

Light

1   Don't take light for granted. Our eyes and brain adapt to the prevailing light so efficiently that we aren't aware of the adjustments they make.

2   The easiest way to become aware of light is to half-close your eyes. This also gives you some idea of how the scene will look on camera by making the shaded parts darker and the light parts lighter.

3   Light is a key to mood. Use it to create atmosphere.

4   Eyes go to the bright parts of the picture first. Before you take a shot, check the viewfinder to make sure the highlights are in the right place. If they aren't, they weaken the shot.

5   Then think about the shadows. They add drama to the picture and are as important for the composition as the bright. Can the dark/bright balance be changed to improve the shot?

6   In low light, use the camera's built-in light booster, known as gain. The benefits of gain are offset by loss of picture quality. At low levels of gain the 'noise' in the dark areas of the picture may be acceptable. At higher levels the picture may look like it was shot in a blizzard.

7   Use the available light creatively. For ideas on how to do this, look again at *Use light and shadow* on page 40.

Properties and problems of light

Hard or soft?

Hard light produces distinct, hard-edged shadows. Soft light produces indistinct, soft-edged shadows. So use hard light if you want deeper shadows and soft light to lift them.

Contrast

Contrast is the difference between the brightest and darkest parts of a scene. Cameras don't cope with extremes of light as well as eyes, so excessive contrast may not look good on screen.

When there is a lot of sky in a shot - usually because the camera is lower than the subject - you can reduce contrast by raising the camera or by moving the subject in front of a darker background, like a tree or a building.

Or use the neutral density (ND) filter to reduce the light entering the camera and thus shift the contrast between bright and dark to a more acceptable exposure.

Colour temperature

Another phenomenon we aren't normally aware of is the colour of light (known as colour temperature). Daylight is bluish, artificial light is yellowish. Our eyes automatically smooth out the difference, so that most light looks colourless and colours look roughly the same in daylight and artificial light.

White balance

To keep colours constant on screen, you have to set the camera for the prevailing light by adjusting the white balance. The camera can do this automatically, but in any situation where the light is coming from more than one source it's safer to do it manually.

To adjust the white balance manually you need to zoom in on something white (a sheet of paper or a shirt) and press the white balance button. If you do this every time the light changes or you move to a new location, all the colours (not just white) will be recorded correctly.

Mixed light

What happens if you have daylight and artificial light in the same shot - if, for example, you are using lights in a room and daylight is coming through a window in the background?

Various solutions:

- **Easy (1)** Draw the curtains to exclude the daylight.

- **Easy (2)** Move your subject so there isn't a window in the background.

- **Less easy** Put blue filters on the lamps so their light matches the daylight. This reduces the area they can light and you may need extra lamps to compensate.

- **Time-consuming** Put orange filters over the window(s) so that the daylight coming in matches the artificial light inside.

- **Handy** Use an HMI, CSI or MSR lamp. These produce light that is the same colour temperature as daylight.

Sound

Don't neglect sound. Viewers will put up with lousy pictures - they might even consider them artistic. But if they can't hear what is being said, they will switch channels.

It's also worth remembering that a large number of people have less than perfect hearing. Older people, for example, have difficulty coping with the cocktail party problem - singling out the voice they want from the general babble. They also struggle to understand speech if background music or sound effects are competing with the words, or if they can't see the speaker. Older people watch a lot of television. Don't neglect their needs.

One other point. Cameras are sold on picture quality. The ads rarely mention sound, even though far more shots are unusable because the sound - not the pictures - is substandard. The sound equipment and controls on many cameras are inferior and difficult to use.

So if you are shooting solo, get someone to help by keeping the mic close to the person who is talking and keeping an eye on the volume level, preferably with a pair of headphones and an external mixer. In fact, you need a sound recordist! If you don't have one, even someone who has been shown only the basics can make the difference between a failed and a successful shoot.

Before you start shooting

1   Stop and listen. Ears interpret (just like eyes), so it's easy to miss how noisy the location background really is. Ears can choose what to listen to; microphones can't.

2   Invest in a decent pair of headphones. Headphones let you hear what microphones pick up, as opposed to what your ears choose to listen to.

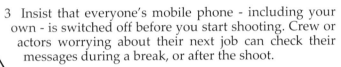

3 Insist that everyone's mobile phone - including your own - is switched off before you start shooting. Crew or actors worrying about their next job can check their messages during a break, or after the shoot.

4   Check the voice level of performers and interviewees and adjust the volume and/or position of the mic(s) accordingly. Then do a test recording and play it back to make sure something is going onto the tape. The volume display may be reacting, but that doesn't necessarily mean the sound is being recorded on the tape.

5 Always record sync sound - it doesn't cost extra. Record sync sound even for general shots and shots you intend to overlay with music. If you don't, you may have to use precious editing or dubbing time looking for substitutes to fit to the pictures.

To get good sound

1   Get the mic in close. The speaker's voice will then dominate most background noise. If you keep the mic far away, you make the voice more difficult to hear and it's more likely to be drowned by background noise.

2   Get close, but keep mics out of shot. Mics that get into shot ruin the illusion of real life you are trying to create on screen. The way to avoid getting mics into shot by mistake is to poke the mic into shot before recording starts. Keep pulling it back until you find the edge of frame. Then be careful to stay beyond it.

3   The on-board mic (built into the camera) will record a speaker satisfactorily if conditions are ideal and the speaker is no more than two metres away. It's always safer, however, to use a clip-on personal mic (hide the cable) or a gun mic Use the camera mic mainly for non-specific sound for general shots.

4   Be careful if the speaker is standing in front of a noisy background (e.g. a busy road or building site), where even a highly directional gun mic will pick up more of the background noise than you want. To reduce background noise, get the mic in close, level with the speaker's waist or chest and pointing upwards; or above the speaker, pointing down. Best of all, turn everything round so that the speaker is in front of something quiet like a building and the noise is behind the mic

5   Accept that you may sometimes have to reject a location because it's too noisy. There's no point shooting there if you can't use what you shoot. 'I can fix it in the edit or the dub' is not a realistic option.

6   It's easy to add sound later, but difficult - if not impossible - to drop it.

7   A simple way to improve a noisy or windy location: shield the mic from the source of the noise. Two people can make a shield if they stand shoulder-to-shoulder, as close to the speaker as possible but just out of shot. Cushions, sleeping bags, blankets, anything else to hand (look around you) may also help as a makeshift sound screen.

8   Remember, films are made in the edit suite, not on location. Think of sound recording as collecting the material you will need to build your sound track later.

9   Record a minute or so of wild track or 'atmos', even in very quiet locations (they all sound different). This can be used during postproduction to fill holes in the track when you cut out some unwanted momentary noise such as a cough. Don't leave recording wild tracks to the end of the day. You may run out of time and the background sound may change.

10 Don't talk while the camera is running - yes, that includes you, the director. And don't start talking again the moment the action finishes. Allow two beats before saying 'Cut' so that the editor can time the cut to suit the pace of the film. Better still, let the cameraman decide when to stop recording.

11 Exploit stereo when you have the chance. Often the best way to do this is to use one channel (or pair of channels) to record the main sound and the other to record background (ambient) sound. You can then mix the tracks later. But can your postproduction system handle multi-track?

12 Finally, be aware that good sound makes pictures come alive. It's like adding a fourth dimension to your material.

Lenses

1   Don't play with the zoom. Zooming in and out makes you feel you're doing something while recording, but it doesn't help the film, the editor, the viewer or the battery. Use the zoom to find focus and the right size of shot before you start recording. Then keep your finger off the button and leave it alone.

2   The **depth of field** is the area of the picture in sharp focus. The depth of field is different at both ends of the zoom.

- Zoomed in, the depth of field is narrow. The foreground or background is out of focus and the picture appears flat.
- Zoomed out, the depth of field is wide. Everything beyond the minimum focal distance (about a metre) is in focus.

So **zoom in**:
- to focus the camera. It will then be in focus for any size of shot, provided the distance between camera and subject stays the same.
- to throw focus from foreground to background or vice versa. You may have to move the camera closer to the foreground subject to achieve the effect.

- to make two people confronting each other appear almost on top of each other. To increase the foreshortening, move the camera further away from the subjects to an over-the-shoulder two-shot (O/S 2-S).

And **zoom out**:
- to make two objects appear to be further apart. To intensify the effect, move the camera closer to the foreground subject.
- to stop having to worry about focus. If you want a closer shot, stay zoomed out and move the camera closer to the subject.

3   Distance is relative, not only for lenses. Seen from the moon, the distance between two lampposts 20 paces apart is zero for most practical purposes. You would, for example, allow as long for a trip from the moon to lamppost A as to lamppost B. So

- move the camera further away to make things seem closer to each other.
- move it closer to make things seem further apart.

4 The size of shot affects the apparent speed on screen, depending on the **direction of movement**.

- Zoomed in, runners, cars etc. moving directly towards or away from the camera appear to cover the ground slowly.
- Zoomed out, runners, cars etc. moving directly towards or away from the camera appear to cover the ground faster.
- Zoomed in, runners, cars etc. moving right to left or left to right appear to be travelling very fast (and are difficult to keep in shot because you are using the lens like a telescope).
- Zoomed out, runners, cars etc. moving right to left or left to right appear to travel more slowly.

5 Use the **macro** setting to get large close-ups of really small objects. The macro reduces the minimum focal distance, so the lens can almost touch the subject. The depth of field in macro shots is very narrow indeed and it is almost impossible to zoom or pull focus. (Not all lenses have a macro.)

Techtalk

The **aperture** is the opening that lets light into the lens. The bigger the opening, the more light gets through.

Lenses have an **angle of view** - wide or narrow, The angle of view is inversely related to the **focal length**. This means that:
- the longer the focal length, the narrower the angle of view.
- the shorter the focal length, the wider the angle of view

The relationship is clear when you think about the shape of a telescope. A telescope is long and thin and shows a tiny part of the scene. It has a long focal length and a narrow angle of view. In contrast, a wide-angle lens is short and fat and shows a lot of the scene. It has a short focal length.

The **zoom** is a variable lens that lets you choose the angle of view/focal length. That's what you are doing when you zoom.

f-number If you divide the focal length of a lens (let's say it's 8.5 mm) by its aperture when fully open (let's say it's 5 mm) you arrive at the f-number (in this case it would be f1.7)

Lens speed The f-number gives you the speed of the lens. The smaller the f-number, the faster the lens. This is important, because the faster the lens, the less light it needs to give an acceptable shot.

Ideas

Some suggestions if you are trying to think of ideas or develop ideas for a drama or documentary.

1   Don't start with a blank page. Keep a box or file with newspaper and magazine cuttings of events or incidents or opinions that might come in useful one day. Get in the habit of scanning women's magazines (lots about relationship and personal problems), agony columns and the lifestyle sections in newspapers. They're good places to fish for stories.

2   Listen to TV and radio programmes that are built round contributions from viewers and listeners: *Home Truths*, for example, on BBC Radio 4 offers a feast of human foibles.

3   Make a note of coincidences or misunderstandings or amusing or frightening incidents that you tell someone about at the time and then normally forget. If they are worth recounting at the time, they may be worth incorporating into a programme.

4   If cuttings and reminiscences fail, don't stare into the middle distance, hoping for inspiration. Look through TV schedules, search your bookshelf, read old diaries.

5   Music, photographs, statues, buildings and paintings can also stimulate the imagination. Imagine what life would be like if you found yourself inside one.

6   Another approach that might start something is to take a situation (purgatory or seventh heaven) and then let your characters work out how to wriggle out of it. If you let the characters take over so that you don't know what the ending will be, you may have a page-turner. If it keeps you intrigued, the chances are your viewers will be too.

7   When you're trying to find a story, work in short bursts. Then do something non-cerebral and completely different like tidying up your room or going to the gym. Your subconscious will take over and very often, up pops a useful idea. (Note that leaving your desk is a strategy for finding an idea, not an excuse for avoiding putting pen to paper.)

8   Or go for a walk and look at the people you come across. Make up stories about them. Who are they? What are they doing? Where do they come from? Where are they going? Why? What if?

9   Here's a way of freeing up your thinking.
• Take a stock situation.
• Reverse the roles of the people involved.
• Add an unlikely qualification.
• What if?
• Exaggerate the situation to breaking point - and beyond.
• The best, the worst imaginable.
• Anchor your scenario in an unlikely time or place.

An example.
• Take a stock situation: a man mugs a woman.
• Reverse the roles: a woman mugs the man.
• Unlikely qualification: the woman is in a wheelchair.
• What if? The man realises he knows the woman.
• Exaggerate wildly: the man is mugged five times by five different women (all known, all in wheelchairs?!)
• The best: the man is a martial arts expert.
• The worst: the women are hopeless muggers - except one.
• Unlikely place. The fifth mugging takes place outside a police station.

Ridiculous, I know. But this sort of exercise can be fun, as well as spark off a story.

Scripting drama (the next section) and *Show things happening* on page 80 may also give you some ideas.

Scripting drama

The following approach works for most people, so unless you have reasons for not doing so, it's a good idea to stick with it.

1   Think of the story first.
2   Then write character biographies.
3   Then plot the story in detail by noting the events of each scene on a sticky notelet or postcard.
4   Shuffle the scenes around to find the most interesting order.
5   Write the dialogue last.

Planning the story

1   Think of a good story, a page-turner. If your viewers want to know what happens next, you have a good story.

2   Drama needs action as well as words. So make movies move. Characters should move emotionally. Viewers should be moved.

3   Keep your drama simple, short and affordable. If you are a new writer, no-one is going to bankroll your attempt to remake *War and Peace* or *Gone with the Wind*.

4   Remember everything, including actors and travelling to locations, costs money. So reduce the number of actors and locations and exploit to the full the ones you do include.

5   Base your characters on real people or aspects of real people (suitably disguised, as necessary).

6   Write biographies for your characters. These should contain far more information than viewers need to know. The actors need the background to put flesh on a fictional person. They also help you devise believable reactions to the problems the characters face in your drama.

7   Explore your characters. How would they react to flood or famine, unexpected bereavement or pregnancy, unrequited love or parents divorcing?

8   To create better fiction, study fact. How do real people react when they get good or bad news? Or fall in love? Or find their partner in bed with someone? Fact is often stranger than fiction.

Perfecting the structure

Work hard at getting the story and structure right. If they aren't right, director, performers and editors face an uphill struggle.

1   Start at the heart of the story, not the start. When you have planned your scenes, try dropping the first few and weigh up what you might gain or lose. If your characters are up to their necks in it in the opening scene, your viewers will want to know how they got themselves into such a fine old mess.

2   Each scene should advance or thicken the plot. If it doesn't, drop it.

3   Does your story have a 'when'? The date and time when things happen (on an anniversary, or the day before a character goes into hospital) can add tension, poignancy, irony and more.

4   Does your story have a 'where'? An eye-catching or surprising location can give a powerful and memorable boost.

5   What's the weather like? Climate and weather can affect mood. It's not difficult to suggest by costume, props, lighting and sound effects.

6   Don't forget lighting. Well-chosen lighting (dawn, dusk, night, glare, sunshine through blinds etc.) sets the mood and can transform what is happening.

7   Remember props. They can give powerful clues to character. Cameras also like details. So the worn cover of a diary can convey volumes about the crazed life of the writer, even before we see any of the scrawled entries.

8   Flashback is a useful device, but don't overuse it. It can destroy the thrust of the story.

9   Don't tell the viewers more than they need to know at any particular moment. 'Treat 'em mean to keep 'em keen' works. When viewers care what happens next, they become participants - and approval ratings soar.

Plot points

'Plot points' are essential information viewers need to follow the story. You have to find ways of getting these points across to viewers as painlessly as possible.

1   There are many standard devices. To introduce a character, for example, show him or her telling a receptionist who he is, whom he wants to see and why. Analyse soaps, dramas, films and theatre for examples of how - and how not - to do it.

2   Prune your plot points. You may think that all are essential for building your characters. But are they essential for viewers?

3   Don't try and cram all the plot points into the first few minutes. If they are as vital to the story as you think, they will emerge anyway. Keep your viewers wanting more.

4   Don't tell me, show me. This applies as much to plot points as to film-making. Hiding a newly arrived letter may betray a husband's infidelity as tellingly as any dialogue.

5   Avoid characters telling each other things they already know. For example, a husband telling his wife: 'When I married you at the age of 30 and you were only 21, I knew that you had been married before to a man who didn't love you.'

6   People don't usually talk aloud to themselves (unless they are mad). Most inconvenient for scriptwriters.

7   But people do pour out their hearts (and your plot points) on their mobiles.

8   If you find yourself struggling to put over some vital point, it's often better to use a short subtitle or a few lines of commentary, particularly at the start of a film. There are many examples in well-known films: *Casablanca*, *American Beauty* etc.

9   Make events believable. Why does someone fail to answer the phone? Or drop their purse? Devise a credible reason. A character may drop his wallet because he's carrying too much shopping. Or a cleaner in a mansion may knock over a priceless vase because he's ogling a bikini by the swimming pool.

10   Invent 'business' such as bumping into furniture or losing one's spectacles to make incidents appear natural. Business can convey plot points as well as build character and create dramatic or comic effects.

Writing dialogue

1 Write with a real person or a particular actor in mind, even if you may not be able to book him or her.

2 When you are writing, 'hear' your characters saying the lines. Or say them out loud to yourself.

3 Spoken word order often differs from written word order. Spoken vocabulary is also different: fewer nouns, more verbs, more colloquial. You may write 'What was the name of that man whom you were talking to?' But you'd probably say 'That man - who was he?' Listen to the way people actually speak.

4 Note also that people don't always speak in complete sentences. 'Right?' 'Right.'

5 Leave space between the words. By which I mean, don't write too much dialogue. Use action instead. A look can say: 'I know you. You're lying again.' An actor tearing open a letter, reading it and then sitting down heavily on the steps can tell viewers a lot about what was in the letter.

6 Use stage directions, not dialogue, to describe action.

7 Write for the viewer, not the script reader. In real life a person holding a bottle of wine might offer someone a drink by saying 'Want some?' This looks unimpressive on the page, so a misguided writer might expand it to 'Would you like a glass of wine?' Which isn't needed if you can see he's holding the wine.

8 Remember the script is the recipe, not the meal. (Though if you are trying to raise funds on the strength of a script, it has to look impressive on the page, so overwriting may be in order.)

9 When you are writing, create life, not a script.

10 When you have written your dialogue, read it out loud with a friend and listen to how it sounds. Do people speak like this? Would your characters say this? Don't be frightened to rewrite.

11 Writing a good script is not easy. Don't be downhearted if it takes a long time and you have to sweat.

Scripting

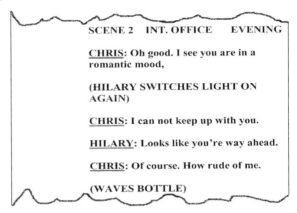

SCENE 2   INT. OFFICE   EVENING

CHRIS: Oh good. I see you are in a
romantic mood,

(HILARY SWITCHES LIGHT ON
AGAIN)

CHRIS: I can not keep up with you.

HILARY: Looks like you're way ahead.

CHRIS: Of course. How rude of me.

(WAVES BOTTLE)

1   You need to make three things clear in your script: who's talking, what they say, and stage directions about movements, settings and props. Decide how you are going to signal each component and then stick to it (e.g. capital letters underlined for names, as normal for dialogue and capitals for stage directions).

2   Don't specify shots in your script. An occasional suggestion, when a shot is vital to the interpretation of a line, is acceptable. But leave the shots to the director. That's his or her job.

Pitching your script

1   Do some research to find the best organisation and the best person in it to send your script to.

2   Write a summary of the story and try it out on a friend. Would he or she want to know more? Attach the summary to your covering letter.

3   Put a footer with © *name and date* at the bottom of each page.

4   Send a copy, not the original script. People lose scripts.

5   Mail the script as a recorded delivery item and keep the post office receipt with the date on it. The © footer and the mailing method will help protect your ideas and script from unacknowledged copying or 'borrowing'.

6   Enclose a s.a.e. so that the script is returned, if rejected.

7   If rejected, ask for feedback so that you can learn.

Working with actors

The scale of the production will obviously affect your way of working with the cast. So adapt the following as time and budget permit.

Casting

1 Choose the right actor for the part and you have done yourself a favour. Don't underestimate the importance of these choices. Later, when a programme is finished, you often realise that its success or failure was determined right at the outset by your casting decisions. This doesn't mean you can blame the actors if things go wrong. You chose them, not vice versa.

2 If you have the money, a casting director is a good investment. He or she can make as much difference to your production as a good cameraman or editor.

3 Treat agents' recommendations with caution. Their job is finding work for their clients, not finding the best performers for your production.

4 Invite actors you are considering to one or more casting sessions. Ask them to bring something of their own choosing so that they can show off their strong points. Also ask them to read one or more parts from your script; you may want to change your mind about the part they play. This lets you and the actors explore possibilities in the script, as well as find the best way of working together.

Prerehearsal

1   Actors need time to prepare. Distribute scripts and character biographies in advance.

2   For smaller productions at least phone to give performers some idea of what they will be asked to do. Particularly if they are likely to get cold or wet or dirty.

3   Work out preliminary ideas for moves for each scene and 'business' (see *Plot points* on page 64). Note moves and business on your director's script in a bird's-eye view diagram or a quick sketch.

Read-through and rehearsal

1   Stage actors can fine-tune their role at every performance. TV and cinema actors don't have that luxury. Don't expect them to get it right without a read-through and rehearsing.

2   At the beginning of a read-through ask each actor to introduce themself briefly, even if some of them know each other already. This gives the new faces a chance to feel part of the team. The faster everyone gets to know each other, the better they will work together.

3   Ask the actors to read their parts aloud from the script. Try to avoid doing a long introduction, directing or interrupting them. Let them interpret their roles in their own way. Listen carefully to their approach and make notes of aspects you like, so that you can integrate them with your ideas about the role.

4   Time this first read-through. If you add time for non-verbal action you will have a rough idea of the eventual duration.

5   When you have read through the whole piece, get the actors to walk through each scene, performing the moves as well as saying the lines. This is when the work of creating the scenes takes place. You need to do this on the location or on a life-size mock-up of it. Use marker tape on the floor to show walls, windows and doors. Use tables, chairs, books and imagination to stand for other items.

6   You may need to do each scene two or three times or more before everyone is happy. If scenes don't work on the ground, they're unlikely to work on camera.

7   Don't let actors overact. Stage actors have to project to the audience. Screen actors have to pull the camera in.

8   Don't demonstrate lines or perform scenes for the actors to copy you. Actors aren't parrots.

9   Stick to the script, unless a suggested change or addition is a definite improvement. It is not a good idea to let an actor ad-lib or paraphrase because he or she hasn't learnt the lines. Respect the writer. If you don't, why are you doing his or her script?

10 Be open to ideas and suggestions, but keep control. Don't let rehearsals or shoots become committee meetings.

11 Make notes on your script of spontaneous reactions, happy accidents, or business that occurs naturally. If they are in the spirit of the script, they may be worth keeping.

12 Don't overrehearse. Get the action to work, but keep it fresh for the camera.

13 Actors love to receive feedback and reassurance. Particularly reassurance. Praise whatever you can before drawing attention to aspects that didn't go so well.

14 If the performance was OK, say so: 'Great!' If you don't, the actors may think you didn't like it and change it next time.

15 If the performance was not OK, make sure your comments are helpful and precise. 'Do it better' is not a helpful comment.

16 Be sensitive to the mood of individuals and of the cast as a whole. You may not be able to iron out every problem you see. If you don't seem to be getting through to an actor, be aware that he or she may also be unhappy. Talk to him privately.

The shoot

1   The actors are the people viewers will see. It's easy to forget this during the shoot, when you are busy with camera, sound, lighting etc. Actors know you have to pay attention to technical details but don't take them too much for granted. Continue to give feedback and reassurance.

2   Introduce them to the crew so that they feel part of the team.

3   When setting up a shot, remind them what happens in the next shot - and in the shot after that, if it affects the way they play the current shot.

4   Show concern for their wellbeing. Make sure they are warm, cool, dry, fed, watered etc.

5   Don't keep actors hanging around unnecessarily. Don't call them before they are needed. If the next shot is going to take 20 minutes to set up, let them take a break. If there is a technical problem, keep them informed.

Continuity

Let's break this topic into three: continuity of direction, continuity of costume and consumables, and continuity of action. Here we will talk about costume, consumables and action; continuity of direction was discussed in *Crossing the line* on page 27.

Why is continuity a problem? The basic reason is that shooting takes longer than viewing. While shots are being lined up on location, the light changes, someone opens a window, a performer unwinds her scarf or unbuttons her jacket. Result: two shots that may look wrong if cut together. If you shoot and show everything live (that is, without stopping) you can't have a continuity problem.

Costume

Costume discontinuities are easy to miss. On any shoot you (or the production assistant) need to look out for the adjustments people make to their clothes between shots, often without thinking. Each of the following has, of course, a reverse, which I haven't listed.

- unbuttoning or unzipping coats and jackets
- taking off coats, hats, gloves
- unwinding, unknotting scarves
- loosening ties
- transferring shoulder bags and handbags to the other side
- rolling up sleeves
- taking off spectacles or sun glasses
- tidying hair

You will have no difficulty adding to this list.

On a programme with days, perhaps weeks, of shooting there is a fresh set of problems. A performer decides to get a haircut or change her hair colour or remove the stubble on his chin.

There is also the problem of what the presenter should wear: one outfit or different outfits? If you and the presenter decide on one outfit, it's sensible to buy at least two identical sets so shooting doesn't have to wait for the laundry. If you decide that different outfits are in order, be aware that there might be a problem if you decide to combine material shot on different days.

Consumables

Smoking and pubs are a continuity minefield. Was the cigarette in or out of shot the last time? In which hand? How long was it? A new cigarette in shot 1 may be a stub by the time you are ready for shot 2.

The pint in the pub can be just as tricky. Give the actor a real one (preferably non-alcoholic) for when you're shooting, and a soft drink for when you're setting up the shot. This protects the continuity on the real drink and keeps the actor sober. It's not unusual for shooting to stretch over several hours, time enough for a thirsty actor to down several pints, which you can be sure won't improve his performance. If the drink is wine or spirits, don't give the actor a real one even for the shoot. Find a non-alcoholic drink that looks similar.

If you want to be hospitable, offer the actors (and the crew) a drink when the shoot is over.

Action

Obviously the most common problem is right hand/left hand.

Continuity is not the most important thing actors have to think about. They need to concentrate - quite rightly - on things like their lines, their timing and so on. Everyone else on the shoot also has more important things to worry about. So it's wholly understandable that an actor changes hands for the close-up of a particular action and no-one notices. Which hand did she use to pick up the paper, unzip the bag, hold the coffee?

It's a good idea to entrust continuity to someone with a sharp eye, a notebook and a good memory: a continuity assistant or, failing that, the long-suffering production assistant. A digital stills camera or Polaroid can also be a great help.

Two-shots

A tricky continuity problem occurs when you use two-shots to cover two people having a conversation in a café or while walking. It's unlikely that the position and action of both people will match in both two-shots, as you will discover in the edit. Hands can be a particular problem.

Cutting between two-shots and single shots is much easier. Or you can avoid the problem to a large extent by using tight over-the-shoulder two-shots that don't show people's arms.

Weather

For example, clouds obscuring the sun. If one shot is taken in bright sunlight and the second when the sun is behind a cloud, the two shots may be unusable together.

Passing aircraft

If you can't wait till they've gone, keep the shot running after the action so that you can fade the noise gently in the dub. The thing to avoid is engine drone that suddenly starts or stops.

Tides

Will the spot you've chosen be under water by the time you've finished? Be aware also of footsteps and tyre tracks on the sand. They can destroy the Robinson Crusoe effect you're after.

Dusk

You're running late and the light is fading fast. Cameras don't compensate for fading light as effectively as your eyes. The scene you're shooting is supposed to take place in daytime. What do you do? The best thing is to cut your losses by covering the remaining action in as few shots as possible.

Finally

Continuity is a minefield, but don't worry about it too much. Viewers aren't looking for mistakes and all but the most glaring will be unnoticed.

If you spot a mistake, work out where viewers will be looking (the part of the screen with the action or the lightest part) and make sure the continuity is right in that part. Few people will notice problems elsewhere.

If there is a discontinuity in the key part of the screen and you can't edit round it, try adding a sudden loud noise like a door slam, or a car horn. It'll distract people's attention. It might even make them blink at the crucial point. Blinking is as good as a blackout for hiding mistakes.

Music and copyright

Music offers a fast track to the thoughts and emotions of both the viewers and the viewed. Use it to make viewers feel happy or sad and to convey what the characters in your programme are thinking. Or use it as counterpoint: sad music over happy pictures, for example, may signal something unpleasant is going to happen.

But music can also harm your programme. Nonstop music telling viewers what to think can infuriate. Overused pieces such as *In an English country garden* or *I do like to be beside the seaside* say more about the producer's lack of imagination than they do about his or her appreciation of music. Hesitate also before you use well-loved masterpieces over your pictures: you may annoy more viewers than you delight. Music is powerful stuff, so choose it carefully.

Other pitfalls to avoid

1   Don't underline the obvious. Do you really need massed violins to ram home the first kiss? Or a tuba to tell people that this scene is funny?

2   Don't use music just to avoid silence. Programme-makers often get nervous if there's a gap in the sound track; viewers find it refreshing. A longer than expected period of silence also makes viewers look at the screen to see why the sound has stopped. So it can be a useful device (often combined with slow motion) for attracting attention to a particularly effective shot.

3   Don't use music to liven up weak shots. Adding music doesn't necessarily strengthen them - you just end up with weak shots with music. It rarely works.

4   Nonstop music in the background can be effective for some types of programme - fashion, for example, which is all about image and being cool. But think carefully before you decide on nonstop music for a programme. Will it really help? Does the easy-listening medley grinding away through your ocean sailing programme add anything? The sound of wind and waves might be far more dramatic and appropriate.

Music *v.* words

If you are thinking of adding loud music under words (commentary, interview or dialogue), think again. Hearing, like eyesight, gets worse as people get older. When this happens it becomes more difficult to tune in to a voice if there's a lot of background noise (the cocktail party problem). Older people watch more TV than the young and regularly complain that they can't hear what's being said. Feedback programmes ignore these complaints most of the time because there is only so much to be said on the subject. But the complaints keep on coming.

Let me end on a more positive note. Music in the right place can be magic, adding a new dimension to your pictures. Just choose your moments - and the music - carefully.

Commissioning music

You might think of getting some music specially written for your programme, perhaps for a single instrument, a guitar or piano or flute - it doesn't have to be for a complete orchestra. If you decide to commission, get the composer in early and show him or her a rough-cut of the programme, suggesting where you think music has a role to play. Fix a fee (does it include repeats?) and let the composer take away a copy of the programme to work to.

Music on a shoot

1   If there is music (TV, radio or disc) playing in the background on a location, ask for it to be switched off. If you need more than one shot to cover the action and you can't have the music switched off (a large hotel, for example, may be wedded to its muzak), you will have to find another location.

2   If you carry on shooting with the music in the background, the music will jump every time you cut. The result will almost certainly be unusable. The way to have music and editability is a) don't have music playing while you are shooting; b) at the end of the shoot make a long continuous recording of it; c) dub it on in postproduction.

3   If you decide in advance that you want to cut a sequence to music, remember that you always need more shots than you think. So shoot plenty. The cameraman should have the music in his or her head while shooting. If possible, get him or her to listen to a recording before the shoot.

Shooting live music

1   If you are shooting a live performance, do a long continuous recording to use as a guide track. Then do all your shots in sync so that you can line them up against the guide track in the edit.

2   Shoot lots of material that isn't so closely linked to any particular part of the music - shots of the audience and the scene in general, close-ups of performers' faces, hands, violin bows, feet tapping etc. Obviously it helps to have more than one camera. If you do, give the operators specific roles: one on the wide safety shots, one on close-ups, one roaming (and keeping out of the other shots).

3   Shooting a live performance becomes easier if you can shoot the same piece twice. If there's only one performance, is it possible to shoot the rehearsal? Are the musicians willing to wear performance clothes for the rehearsal?

4   Remind your cameramen that excessive camera movement can distract from enjoyment of the music. So ask them to try not to spend too much time restlessly searching for ace shots. The music must come first.

5   If you want to do a really good job on filming live music, study the score or a recording and make notes of where the trumpets come in or where the cello has a big moment. You can then make sure the cameras are in the right place at the right time.

Copyright

If you use music in a programme, you need to know what it is and who is performing, so that you can clear the copyright. Some music may not even be clearable. Copyright is a vast and complicated subject and you must seek advice. A good place to start is *www.MCPS-PRS-Alliance.co.uk.*

Editing drama

You need an editor to edit drama well. In fact you need an editor
to edit anything well. There are at least three reasons.

1   Editing is a creative art that goes way beyond knowing how
to operate the equipment. You may be a good director but that
doesn't necessarily mean you are a good editor.

2   The editor brings a fresh eye to your material. The director
knows the history and intention behind each shot and this can't
help influencing his or her assessment of it. The editor sees only
the shot - as viewers do. So his or her judgement isn't
contaminated by what went on during the shoot. This can work
both ways. Some of your most cherished shots may not be as
effective as you hoped. But others may be far more effective.
Trust the editor's judgement.

3   The editor knows how to work the machinery. As
technology develops, it makes more and more things possible
but, inevitably, more features create more complications. Of
course, given time, you can learn to work the machinery, but
you will never become as fast and as proficient as a full-time
editor. Moreover, if you are struggling with the computer, you
can't concentrate on pictures and sound, which are what really
matter. So do yourself a favour by not doing your own editing.

Make a shot list

1   View the material with the editor. Make a shot list, giving
each shot a short name (e.g. arriving) and noting rough time
codes for each take so that you and the editor can find shots
quickly when you need them. Another way of using this
information is to put it on the script as 'tramlines': vertical lines
labelled with shot numbers that run alongside the dialogue
covered by each shot. You and the editor can then see at a glance
how many shots there are for each part of the dialogue.

2   If there are several takes for each shot, view all of them and
decide which one you and the editor prefer. Then give it a
couple of ticks on your list. If you don't do this, you will forget
which was the best take and waste time viewing them again
when it's time to use the shot.

3   If there is a lot of material and you have time to get VHS
copies with burnt-in time codes, go through the material in
advance by yourself and identify the material that obviously
won't make the final show. Don't prune too hard. If a shot might
be useful, digitise it.

Procedure for editing drama

1   Make a first assembly of the material as scripted.

2   View the assembly. Have you started at the heart of the story, not the start? Would you lose anything if you dropped one of the opening scenes?

3   Note where the drama slows or drags. These sluggish patches are often a sign of overwriting. If a line or chunk of dialogue won't be missed, drop it.

4   Have you shown words or action twice?

5   Look at the way each section or line of dialogue is covered on screen. The person who is speaking doesn't always have to be on screen while he or she is speaking. The shot of the listener may be more revealing. Who does the viewer want to see?

6   Don't chop the story into lots of little bits just because you have the shots to do so. If the actors are working well together and their timing is good, keep shots running until there is a solid reason to cut.

7   Do the shot sizes reflect the intensity of the drama?

8   Trim shots carefully. A few frames more or fewer can make a huge difference to the success of a cut and the pace of the film.

9   Remember the need-to-know principle. This is a useful concept to have in mind when planning, shooting and editing. Don't show or tell viewers more than they need to know at any stage in the story. Postponing gratification keeps them interested and gives you the chance of springing a few surprises. Close-ups, camera angles and light can all be used to keep viewers guessing.

10 Don't get too preoccupied with continuity. If head and arm positions don't match perfectly from one shot to the next, work out which part of the screen viewers are focused on and make sure the continuity is right in that part. If viewers are actively engaged in the drama, discontinuities in less important parts of the screen will probably go unnoticed.

11 The size of the screen your drama plays on affects whether it feels fast or slow. Larger screens show more detail, so the cutting pace can be slower. On a small screen, however, viewers can see less detail, so they take in a shot more quickly. Unless you're making a feature film, cut tight.

The points in *Editing basics* on page 34 and *Editing factual programmes* on page 103 are also relevant for editing drama.

Factual Programmes

Factual programmes key concept

Show things happening

Here's a recipe for a factual programme or documentary. Write a commentary (or narration or script or voice-over - whatever you want to call it). Interview some people to flesh out the commentary and shoot some pictures to illustrate it. Edit to taste. And you have a documentary.

Do you? What you have is a slide show, a radio programme with pictures. As a TV programme it's - well - dead. That's because 80% of the message is in the words. Virtually nothing happens in the pictures. They're just filler.

It should, of course, be the other way round. The weight of the message should be in the pictures, with the words filling in the details and presenting the abstract ideas that are difficult for pictures to communicate. That's why the key concept for this section is show things happening.

In factual programmes or documentaries this can be difficult. Drama is fiction, so you have complete control. You decide what is going to happen, put it in the script and make it happen in front of the camera. Documentary events, on the other hand, are more awkward to capture on camera. They happen at inconvenient times and in unattainable places. So you have to resort to narration and interviewees talking about events. Too many interviewees, too much narration and too few pictures of things happening and you are in trouble.

How to show things happening

1 Don't write a script in advance. Write a treatment (as described in the *Planning with a treatment* on page 94).

2 Choose a good story that makes a film you yourself would want to watch. It should be a story you would want to tell someone about, even if you weren't making the film. A story that makes you wonder 'How did it happen?' or 'What happens next?'

3 Choose people. Stories about people are what you, I and other people are most interested in: their experiences and ideas, their lives and their loves, how they got themselves into a particular situation, how they get out of it, how they react to good or bad fortune, how they cope with stress, mishap, crime, wealth, poverty, a demanding job, love or the lack of it.

4 The time to make a documentary about a person or group of people is when things are changing, because that's when there are events and developments for your camera to record. Things change when people are directly affected by world events; or chuck in their job; or join a gym; or volunteer to work for a charity; or decide to find a home help for the baby and go back to work; or build a new lifestyle by getting professional advice on diet, make-up or allergies.

5 Another approach is to make things happen. You might take a person or a group of people and follow them through an experience, like living on a desert island or crewing a sailing ship or swapping jobs. On a less ambitious level you might try getting owners of unruly dogs to take their pets to a training class or animal therapist; or follow smokers or drinkers trying to give up; or getting friends to road-test the local dating agencies.

6 Of course, you can't always be there when something happens. An interviewee reliving or describing or reacting to the experience can be almost as good (if possible, do the interview where the event took place). Re-enactments have also become commonplace in factual programmes. But footage of the actual event is always preferable.

7 Avoid worthy, unvisual and abstract subjects that focus not on people but on institutions or organisations or concepts such as national unity. If you are asked to make such a film, centre it on one or two of the people involved rather than the institution or concept. This usually makes a far better film.

8   Don't try and make the definitive story about anything. TV is not an encyclopaedia. Factual programmes can illuminate a subject by highlighting certain aspects but a comprehensive list of all the facts is not what TV is good at.

9   Go easy on dates and statistics. Viewers won't remember more than a couple. Many more and you're probably neglecting the events and experiences that make good television.

Ethics

The question that soon comes up when you are trying to show things happening is 'How much is it ethical to fix?' Your station may have guidelines, but for many situations you will have to find your own boundary between fixing and faking.

For me the boundary is defined by routine and emotion.

I think it's perfectly acceptable to ask people, for the purposes of a film, to take the children to the playground or drive to work or feed the chickens, provided this is part of their normal life. For an action that is not routine but a one-off (like having a flat tyre, riding a bicycle in an evening dress or locking oneself out of the house), I think you are on tricky ground if you pretend a re-creation is the actual event. But there's no reason why you shouldn't use a re-creation to illustrate someone describing the event in interview or voice-over.

You are also crossing the boundary if you ask someone to re-create an emotional event - like getting the results of the medical test, or learning they've got a place at university or been accepted for military service. Faking emotion is work for actors and you should use actors to do it, not your factual contributors. Instead, film your subjects telling you what happened, what it meant to them and what they did when the news came, preferably in the place where it actually happened. Relating an experience may make interviewees relive it. Even with restrained interviewees, the emotion should come across.

Factual programmes project

Objective

Shoot and edit a short factual story (a short documentary) that shows things happening.

Shooting time

At least 3 hours, if you are on a training course. If you are not on a course, you can allow yourself longer - perhaps a day. But don't go overboard and give yourself a week to shoot this project. This is a practice shoot and you will learn as much from a film that takes a day to shoot as you will from one that takes a week.

Editing time

Editing factual programmes always takes longer than editing drama because you aren't tied to a script. So you will need 2-3 times the shooting time with an experienced editor to arrive at a good rough-cut. If you are operating the equipment yourself, you will need longer.

Duration

Anything between 2½ minutes and 4 minutes for a 3 hour shoot, but the duration is not the objective. Concentrate on making the story as effective as possible, not the duration.

Location

Any convenient and cooperative place or group of people where there is enough activity or development to show things happening.

Cast

Possibly a presenter or on-screen interviewer, but preferably not. Though presenters and interviewers are invaluable for some programmes, their presence for this exercise takes the emphasis away from showing things happening. If you decide to use a presenter, see *Presenters* on page 100.

Planning

The first step is to find a subject or story that gives you the chance to show things happening. You should have some ideas jotted down in a notebook or a press cuttings file that will start you researching a few possibilities (see *Ideas* on page 60 and *Research* on page 89). If you are making the factual programme for a training exercise, the local railway fanatic or fire station or animal rescue centre often makes a good subject.

A visit to the potential location (see *Recce* on page 88) is needed before you can decide to go ahead. Check how much scope the location gives you to show things happening before you make your final decision.

When you have chosen what to film, you have to decide how to film it - in other words, choose a shooting style. *Approaches* on page 90 gives you some ideas. This stage - finding a televisual way to tell the story - is often the most difficult. You may have an excellent subject on an excellent location but how do you turn these assets into something that suits the screen? What is the story?

You then need to do a treatment - see *Planning with a treatment* on page 94. The last step in the planning process is to see whether you can afford the film -*Time and money* on page 120 gives you a way of estimating costs.

Hints

The key concept in the *Storytelling* section (shooting is collecting pictures and sound for editing) stressed the importance of good coverage to provide the editor with material he or she can do something with. The *Drama* key concept (shoot for the screen) encouraged you to work hard on the pictures.

Good coverage and picture quality are just as important for factual programmes.

Your **coverage** needs to be full enough to allow restructuring in the edit suite. Because factual storylines tend to be less rigid, they can often be restructured more radically than drama.

As for **picture quality**, if you're covering riot or mayhem, it may be acceptable to have grainy, out-of-focus, poorly composed pictures. They might even add to the drama of the situation.

But riot and mayhem are very much the exception. Away from the danger zone **good photography** is a must. Pointing the camera vaguely in the right direction isn't enough to give you good pictures. Can you improve the shot by changing camera position, height, angle or shot size? Can you close a curtain or shut a door or rig a lamp to make better use of the available light? Or modify the action for the camera? If you want good photography, you have to keep trying. See *Looking for good shots* on page 47 and *Composition* on page 50.

One point about documentaries that is often forgotten is that you can use all the **cinematic techniques** you used in drama, except for making things up. Suspense, flashback or forward, montage, slow motion or speeded-up shots, freeze frames, exploiting depth of field, contrast and focus are just as valid for documentaries. Use them imaginatively and people will start to call you a film-maker.

You are inevitably going to do **interviews** for your documentary. *Interviews* on page 96 gives you ideas for making these as lively as possible. Here I just want to draw attention to the danger of making extended use of interviewee words as commentary or voice-over and cutting the pictures to fit the words. This is simply another form of the write-the-script-first technique. For short sections the technique works. But if you use it for longer passages you come up against the fact that words and pictures work at different speeds.

You might, for example, interview a farmer about her daily routine and she might say 'I get up at 5.30 and feed the chickens and then make breakfast'. The pictures of her feeding the hens at dawn and then making breakfast will be worth far more time on screen than the time taken to say the words. You will be missing a lot if you let the words dictate the duration of the pictures. **Cut the pictures first**; then fit the words to the pictures - if you still need the words. In this example you probably don't. The pictures say it all.

Cutting the pictures first not only produces better results, it's also easier, because fitting words to pictures is easier than fitting pictures to words. Furthermore, if you use interviewee words as voice-over, you are free to edit them as you wish because you don't have to worry about the picture jumping. So take the opportunity of cutting out hesitations, repetitions and digressions to make the words flow more smoothly.

Research

If you want to make a successful documentary you need to do some research. Don't assume you know all about - for example - firefighters just because you have seen them on the news. You need to find out who they are, why they are in the fire service, what they do most of the time (fighting fires is not the answer). If you aren't curious about them and don't have questions to ask, you probably shouldn't be making a film about them.

Your research should be in two parts - off and on location.

Off location

The obvious place to start researching is on the web. Start with a general search. This will come up with an unmanageably huge number of leads: a good search engine will produce more than a million for 'firefighters'. But take a quick look through the first few pages gives you a feel for what's available. If you haven't already done so, read through the tips for the search engine you are using. Then start refining your searches to - say - 'firefighter psychology'. The more specific the search criteria, the more useful the results. Three criteria in the search box, 'firefighter psychology motive', may give you some really interesting leads. Whatever the results, you will get lots of ideas for aspects to explore when you start talking to real firefighters.

It's also worth checking the Amazon website to find out what's been written on the subject and paying a visit to the local bookshop. For a quick overview of your subject, encyclopaedias (web or printed) are not to be despised. All the above can take place in between talking to people on the phone: current and former firefighters , people who've suffered fires etc.

You have to make a judgement when is the best time to mention the fee (or absence of fee). Don't leave it to an afterthought. The best approach is to let the location know as early as possible who you are making the film for and how long you are likely to be on the location. Then offer them a fee - or nothing, if that is what you have in mind. This avoids unpleasant surprises for both you and your subjects.

How much time you devote to this off-location research and preparation depends, of course, on the time available and the sort of film you want to make.

On location

On-location research is a mixture of meeting your subjects face-to-face and the recce (checking the technical details you need for filming). See the next section.

1   Talk to anyone on the location who may be useful (not just firefighters). The caretaker or dinner lady may have interesting things to say.

2   Ask about routine events (professional training, fitness training, meals, cleaning, recreation) and not-so-routine events (outside inspections, fitness checks). Decide which activities are most likely to yield pictures that combine interest and insight.

3   For activities you have chosen, find out when and where they take place, the detail of what will happen, and what happens when the activities are over. Start thinking about camera positions and shots.

4   Remember that the starting times you are given may not be accurate. Late starts aren't the problem - you're there, ready and waiting. Early starts, however, can be a disaster.

5   Decide whom you want to interview. Spend some time with them to build up their trust. The stronger the bond you build, the better they will perform. At the end of this process, confirm what they have agreed to do, where and when.

6   Look for objects, signs and details that convey the flavour of the location. Rows of helmets, boots, axes, girlie calendars, newspapers, magazines, notice boards, signs and other paraphernalia such as overflowing ashtrays and leftovers after lunch can build up a revealing portrait of your subject.

7   Don't try and make reality conform to received wisdom (e.g. firefighters hate fires). Keep an open mind. The truth is frequently more interesting than preconceived notions.

8   Who? What? Where? When? Make sure that everyone knows the activities and interviews you want to film, where you want to film them and when.

9   You may find it difficult to make up your mind about all these things while actually on the location. There's nothing to stop you giving a rough indication of what you are likely to go for and then phoning later to confirm your plans. This will give you time to think about your approach to the story. See *Approaches* on page 90.

Recce

For all but the simplest films it's advisable - time and budget permitting - to make a second visit after the on-location research, preferably with the cameraman. Use this visit to check on technical details and think ahead about camera positions and possible problems for **camera**, **sound**, **safety** and **production**.

Camera

1   Will you need any special equipment: extra lenses, filters, camera mounts or tracks, small tripods (baby legs)?

2   Will the sun and shade be in the right place when you want to film?

3   Do you need extra lights? If so, how many?

4   Is there sufficient electricity for the lights? Will you have to pay extra for it?

5   Where can you recharge batteries?

6   Will computer screens be stable in your shots?

Sound

1   Will traffic noise make life difficult? Is there anything you can do about it?

2   Are noisy activities such as mowing the lawn or digging up the road with pneumatic drills planned for the shooting day? Can they be rescheduled?

3   Will the builders and carpenters still be working next door? Where is that circular-saw noise coming from?

4   Are there local airports, heliports, military bases, flying clubs that may burst into activity on the day you are shooting? Will they interfere with radio mics?

5   Can muzak, public address systems and noisy fridges or air conditioning be switched off while you are filming?

Safety

1   Ask the people on location if there are any potential hazards such as radiation or fumes.

2   Also do your own assessment. Familiarity can make people underrate danger, sometimes catastrophically. A zoo keeper, for example, can easily forget how dangerous his animals are and how dangerous they can become when their routine is disrupted by strangers with unusual equipment.

3   Will you need any special equipment: helmets, harnesses, protective clothing, buoyancy gear? Can the location provide it?

4   What measures can the location take to ensure safety during the shoot?

5   If you are planning high shots, are the vantage points and the means of access safe? Is a special safety harness needed? Who is going to provide it? (Check also that the cameraman is willing to shoot from heights and is insured to do so.)

Production

1   Do you need to ask someone senior (possibly not on site) for permission to shoot? Head office or landlords or parents?

2   Who has the keys if you want open a gate or move a vehicle or do a shot from the roof?

3   Do you need to provide your own refreshments (tea, coffee and water)? Where can you have lunch? Where are the toilets?

4   Parking. You may need two areas: one nearby to access equipment quickly during the shoot, one for personal transport.

5   The crew will need address and phone numbers for the location and main contact there, your mobile and fixed phone numbers, a sketch map and travel instructions. Can you provide the information required?

6   Crew clothing. Is anything out of the ordinary required? Are they likely to get dirty? Or are formal suits needed?

7   Will you need cash to pay contributors, fees, taxis and other out-of-pocket expenses? Cheques are obviously safer but cash is more convenient. Take a receipt pad for recipients to sign.

8   Are there any eye-catching scenes you could use to publicise your film? Will you need a stills photographer?

Approaches

One of the great joys of TV is that it offers you a range of ways to tell a story, many of them unique to the medium. It's easy to forget just how wide the range is when your head is full of shot lists, timetables, transport, parking and other things that need to be sorted out for the shoot. This section is designed to remind you of some of the possibilities.

It also encourages you once again to find a picture-driven - as opposed to a word-driven - way of telling your story. A word-led way to start your film might be to show a presenter standing next to a sign at the entrance to a location. He tells viewers what the location is, when it first opened, what it does, and then invites us to go inside. This would make a less than inspiring opening in print. It's dire as TV.

There must be a better way.

Seeing and hearing
1   Adopt a distinct point-of-view (POV). Perhaps see your story through the eyes of one of the characters involved: a child, animal, patient, victim, official or loser. A child's-eye view, for example might involve keeping the camera at knee-height or below.

2   The Nepalese POV. If you made a film in an exotic country like Nepal, many things would look strange, and therefore worthy of a shot. See your story as a Nepalese TV director might, recognising that the commonplace here may also look strange.

3   Look round where you are shooting and ask yourself which details express the uniqueness of the location or the people in it. What should you show the viewers to convey the essence of the place? Look at things like ashtrays, calendars, pictures, notes next to the phone, objects on the mantlepiece, books, pets etc.

4   Close your eyes and listen. Imagine that you are making a sound portrait of the location. Which noises would you choose to characterise it?

5   Would it help to see the story through the eyes of an on-screen interviewer or presenter?

Structure

1   Do the story as an investigation, perhaps by the police or a private eye.

2   Do the story as a tongue-in-cheek investigation, in the style of bumbling Inspector Clouseau or mega-cool Philip Marlowe.

3   Perhaps your efforts to get the story are the story.

4   Or you might shoot the story as a video diary.

5   Contrast someone's official job with what he or she thinks about it privately. The discrepancies can be interesting.

6   A life in the day of someone…

7   Fly on the wall. Build up a portrait of an institution or community by recording observational sequences of what goes on. Note, however, that successful fly-on-the-wall programmes usually need many hours of shooting.

8   Sometimes one detail can give you the structure for a whole film. A restaurant can be defined by the menu and what people order from it. A prayer board where people request intercession for the sick or troubled can give you a insight into the life of a church or cathedral.

9   Some films are notoriously difficult to structure: films about architecture or exhibitions of things that don't move (paintings, sculpture, design or snuff boxes). The architect, artist or designer is usually dead. Sometimes visitors talking about their favourite object or what they found most eye-opening in the exhibition are more illuminating than the experts.

10 With difficult subjects don't try too desperately to compensate for the lack of movement or pictures by hiring a celebrity presenter and dressing up him or her as Mickey Mouse. Dumbing down a subject is guaranteed to fail: soap fans and sports addicts won't watch anyway and viewers who are interested will feel patronised.

11 Stay true to your subject. Being true to your subject, however, doesn't excuse you from making the programme appeal to as wide an audience as possible. Aim to be popular as well as true.

Devices

1   **Montage** Take close-ups of each step in a procedure, like getting dressed for a special event or locking up before going out. Then cut the shots together into a fast-moving montage.

2   **Speed up** or **slow down** shots (during the edit, not when shooting).

3   **Time lapse** Set the camera to take one frame every x second.

4   **Vox pop** Record a succession of different people reacting to the same question or situation (e.g. Does giving money to beggars help them?) Cut together, using the question only once.

5   **Locked-off shots** Put the camera on a tripod and position it to do an interview or vox pop against a static background. Then lock it off and make sure you don't move it. Shoot the static background without anyone in shot. Then interview people as usual, but without moving the camera. Cut or mix between sound bites during the edit to make interviewees appear and disappear as if by magic. This device can also be used to denote the passing of time: for example, use a high-angle locked-off shot of a dinner table with full, and then with empty, plates.

6   Ask interviewees to talk **directly to the camera**. This works better if the statements are short. For longer contributions interview in the normal way.

7   Some **combination** of vox pop, locked-off and straight-to-camera interviews. Perhaps have people do a vox pop straight to camera. Or do straight-to-camera locked-off interviews.

8   **Whip pan** Swing the camera as fast as possible from one object to another so that the area in between is a blur. In the edit do fast mixes during the blurs to give your film a different feel.

9   **Cut shots to music** If possible, play the music to the cameraman in advance so that he or she can match the rhythm of the shots with the music. For a short film on a picture-rich location consider setting the whole film to music. If you do this, make sure you shoot plenty of material.

10 **Juxtaposition** Look out for pictures or events that can be juxtaposed with each other: for example, commuter stress contrasted with a little pre-dinner putting practice on a country golf course. Or juxtapose pictures and sound: peaceful music with stressful shots, blues with happy occasions.

Looks and a role for the camera

Your cameraman will love you if you have thought about the way you want your pictures to look.

- Gritty, handheld realism?
- Romantic softness?
- Hard-edged, high-tech brightness?

Also, what role do you want the camera to play?
- Intrusive?
- Detached observer?
- Active handheld participant?
- Artist's impression?

Is the chosen role appropriate? Why?

Watch

Events during the shoot can often reveal character traits or suggest leads that are worth pursuing and capturing on camera. So be sensitive to:

- How contributors sit, stand and behave when they're not on camera.
- How contributors change when you start shooting.
- What contributors do and say after you say 'Cut'.

As a result of your observations you may decide to turn off the record light on the front of the camera and start recording before contributors are 'ready'.

If you are not shooting fly-on-the-wall, this can be a betrayal of trust. Is it ethical? Will the contributors feel tricked? Will they mind?

Remember

Shoot a grabby opening shot or sequence to get viewers interested. Set up something special but be prepared to change your mind in the cutting room if a better opening shot presents itself.

Planning with a treatment

Why do a treatment? You've chosen your subject, you've done the research and recce and you've decided on an approach or a combination of approaches. Why don't you just make the arrangements for the shoot and turn up and shoot what's there?

Shooting what's there is great for a webcam, or if you (and your subjects) have unlimited time, money and patience. On most shoots, however, time, money and patience are limited. You need structure and discipline to make a successful film. That's what the treatment helps to provide.

It's basically a list of the events or sequences in the order that you think they will appear in the completed film. Put a short description of the event or sequence in the left-hand column and summary of the commentary, interviews and other sound in the column on the right.

Once you have done the treatment you can use it to answer some important questions.

Do I have a film?

If the answer is 'No', the doubts will start to surface when you are doing the treatment.

If the left-hand column is just interview interspersed with general shots of traffic, your film will look as thin on paper as it would on screen - unless the interview(s) are riveting.

If your treatment survives this first test, check for predictability, content, and impact. If your film doesn't offer viewers anything new or the chance to share an experience, you probably don't have a film. Think again what the film is really about and how you can make it work.

Who is the film for?

Obviously you want every available viewer to watch your film but in a multi-channel industry, that's an unrealistic target. Think hard about whom your film is for, because you can then make assumptions about what target viewers might already know about the subject, what they might be interested in and how much depth they would welcome.

Am I doing justice to the subject?

The trap to avoid is making a film about something like code breaking and never explaining any of the techniques because you think they are too complicated. That way, you end up with a film that says code breakers are clever (which everyone knew) and little else. So viewers who already know something about the subject, learn nothing. Less informed viewers are also disappointed, because they learn little. And viewers who aren't interested in code breaking, don't watch. Failure all round.

With a complicated subject, aim to delight core viewers but also make it understandable for the less informed. Viewers don't mind being out of their depth occasionally if they enjoy the programme as a whole.

Does the film show things happening?

If it doesn't, check through your notes to see whether you missed anything that might make a good sequence.

Where are the weaknesses?

Identify areas where you are short of material. Is there anything you can do to improve things? Is another sequence or graphics or library material called for? Have you missed anything?

Will the film be long enough?

Jot down how long each sequence in the treatment might run. With any luck your guesses over and under will cancel out. If you don't have a feel for durations, time some sequences in a programme similar to yours. Plan enough sequences to overrun by 10-20%. Being spoilt for choice in the edit suite is better than having to stretch thin material to fill a slot.

How long will it take to shoot?

See *Time and money* on page 120.

Which are the key sequences that must be shot?

Highlight the sequences that are essential to the story. The final scene is usually the one that suffers when you run out of shooting time - a pity, as it's also one of the most important. Make sure you leave enough time to do it justice.

Is the treatment a straitjacket?

A treatment is a preproduction plan that can be overtaken by events. If it is overtaken, go with the events. You probably got lucky because you worked out a good plan.

Interviews

The best advice for shooting interviews is keep it simple. A medium close-up (MCU), showing head and shoulders down to the armpits, is always appropriate. It's close enough to keep on screen as long as you want, without being so close that it's intrusive.

If you keep to an MCU for the whole interview, you can also edit according to the content of the interview, without worrying about camera movements. And if your programme is going to be sold abroad, the MCU, unlike closer shots, has enough room at the bottom for subtitles.

But the most important benefit of keeping it simple is that it allows you to concentrate on getting the optimum performance from your interviewee. Most people become tense when they are being filmed. This may help them give a good performance - or it may not. If the nerves show, the best thing to do is carry on for a few minutes until the interviewee settles down and then stop recording. When the camera stops running, the pressure is off, sometimes visibly. Reassure the interviewee that all is well and start again from the top. With luck, the pressure stays off.

If your performer doesn't relax when the camera is off, you have problems. Sometimes shooting a 'rehearsal' produces good results. Interviewees rarely object if you use a bit of subterfuge to help them perform better on screen.

Location

It's worth working hard to find the best place to do an interview. The formality of the sitting room or manager's office often inhibits speakers. During the recce or while the crew is setting up, notice where the interviewee is most at ease and therefore most ready to confide. Or you can try doing parts of the interview in different places. If the interviewee is particularly at ease in one of these places, there's nothing to stop you repeating questions you covered in previous positions. In fact why not do the whole interview there?

Sometimes it can be appropriate to take an interviewee away from his or her normal surroundings - to an empty playground, for example, to talk about childlessness (if the interviewee doesn't find it too distressing).

Prompts instead of questions

You have to decide before starting an interview whether you want questions in the final programme. If you don't want questions (the easiest way), you don't need to ask them. Instead you just feed the interviewee prompts for the next topic or anecdote: 'What about the..?' or 'Tell me...' As there's no question, the interviewee won't start with 'Yes' or 'No'.

If you can encourage the interviewee to name the subject in his or her answer ('The meeting was a disaster...') rather than refer to it with a pronoun ('It was a disaster...') you will find you can use the answer as a self-explanatory sound bite without having to set up the subject in the commentary.

Interviewees often have a problem understanding why they need to name the subject at the beginning of an answer. If they don't understand, it's easier to stop explaining and start recording. If the interviewee starts without the subject ('It was a disaster...'), gently interrupt and ask him or her to rephrase: 'Could you start with "The meeting was a disaster..."'

Recording questions

If you decide to record questions, make sure they are recorded at the same volume as the answers. The interviewer may also have to appear on screen at some point. For this you will need two-shots (showing interviewer and interviewee), 'noddies' and cutaway questions (shots of the interviewer repeating key questions). Things are getting more complicated.

It's worth thinking about how the interviewee and interviewer should sit or stand in relation to each other. Side by side, at right angles or facing each other? It depends on the subject matter.

Group interviews

If you are shooting a group discussion, it can be difficult to catch each person's opening words on camera. If a member of the group wants to say something, signal with your hand to ask him or her to wait until the cameraman finds the shot. This give you clean editing points.

To edit a group interview you also need cutaways of the participants listening to each other. When you are shooting cutaways, interviewees are often more relaxed and revealing, so it can be worth reshooting parts of the discussion. If you warn camera and sound that you may do this, they can quietly switch to recording speakers rather than cutaways.

Before the interview

1   Avoid giving questions in advance to interviewees, specially written ones. People who want written questions usually prepare written answers. Instead of good talk, they deliver wordy essays.

2   Run through the topics you want to raise with the interviewee and assess his or her answers. This establishes what the interviewee can - or is willing to - talk about. You may discover that you are talking to the wrong person!

3   If you are using an interviewer, let him or her conduct this run-through with the interviewee. This give both parties a chance to bond before the recording.

4   Don't let the run-through become a rehearsal so that the performance sounds second-hand. If the interviewee insists on going through word-by-word, you might as well shoot the 'rehearsal'. You can record it again if you need to.

Shooting

1   Ask the interviewer to stand next to the camera. This gives a full-face shot of the interviewee.

2   Ask the interviewee to talk to the interviewer only. If the interviewee's eyes are flicking between interviewer and crew because he doesn't know where to look, he will appear shifty on screen.

3   Don't shine lights in the interviewee's eyes.

4   Don't yell 'Action' and 'Cut'. Say them quietly - or just nod an OK.

5   Don't clap the clapperboard in the interviewee's face.

6   Keep yourself and the crew out of the interviewee's eye line. If this isn't possible, avoid looking directly at the interviewee. Watch the monitor instead. Ideally, the only person the interviewee should be aware of is the interviewer.

7   When you stop recording, make sure you say something encouraging to the interviewee before you talk to the crew.

8   Remember, interviewee, interviewer and you all have the same goal: a good interview. So be understanding and considerate of the needs of the performers.

If you are the interviewer

1   Don't write out the questions. A list of key phrases should be enough to suggest questions that reflect what has already been said. This stops your questions sounding stilted.

2   Ask one question at a time.

3   Make sure that you keep eye contact with the interviewee. Look relaxed and keep encouraging him or her by looking interested and nodding more than you would in a normal conversation.

4   Make sure any encouragement is silent. Off-camera yeses, or grunts of approval can be difficult to cut out in the edit.

5   Invite the interviewee to start an answer again if it went wrong or was not as good as it could be. You can keep the camera running while you do this (unless the problem needs discussion to be resolved).

6   Don't be too quick with prompts or questions at the end of answers. Leave a gap (long enough to take a breath) to make editing easier.

7   Use silence. If you pause at the end of an answer as if you are expecting more, the interviewee will often give you more. These afterthoughts, because they're spontaneous, may be revealing.

8   If you use questions (rather than 'What can you say about..?' or 'Tell me...') adopt a position of informed ignorance. If you sound less informed than you really are, the answers will be right for viewers. They haven't done the homework. Some interviewers claim they never ask a question they don't know the answer to.

9   Avoid being excessively deferential. The 'thanks to your wise leadership...' approach isn't helpful to the interviewee or you. If he agrees, he sounds complacent. If he doesn't agree, he may come over as falsely modest. And you sound servile.

10 Make questions sceptical or challenging. But don't be aggressive. Leave confrontational interviewing to the celebrity specialists. Would they get more informative answers and higher-profile interviewees if they were less savage? As Michael Parkinson said - talking about his chat show, but it holds for other types of programme: 'You don't have to have blood on the carpet for a good interview'.

Presenters

Producing presenters

The first thing to realise about presenters is that they often feel left out of things, a semi-detached member of the production team.

Semi-detached? Surely not. The person whose face the viewers see? Whose name is featured in the title?

But presenters often do feel left out. Most of the important decisions are made well before recording day. That's as it should be: I'm not advocating that production decisions should be delayed so that presenters can be consulted. But when the presenter does finally arrive on the scene, he or she may be faced with an inflexible plan produced by a team which has already bonded. The presenter doesn't feel part of the team. Not a good start for someone who wants to shine for your programme - and for his or her career.

So how do you make a presenter feel included? Tell him or her what's being planned a few days before he joins the production. When he arrives in the office or on location, make him welcome. Introduce him to the team. Make a bit of a fuss of him. And - this is the key bit - keep him informed about what's going on.

Presenters on location

You are working on a holiday show and have decided to hire a travel writer to front a report. The writer knows she's been hired, but a few days before she's due on location she still doesn't know what the report is about and what she's supposed to wear, let alone if there's a clothes allowance. You are already on location with the team and everyone is too busy to give her a call. She's tried phoning the production office but they have only a rough idea of what you're up to and can't answer her questions. They promise to talk to you and get back. But they are busy and forget to do so.

Eventually the presenter flies out to join you. You meet her in the hotel bar and welcome her (you get that bit right). You brief her about the story, explain tomorrow's shoot and give her the script for her statements to camera.

'Do you mind if I rewrite to suit my way of talking?'

'OK, if you must. But we've worked out the shots, so please change as little as possible.'

Next day the shooting takes longer than expected and it's late afternoon before you get to the statements to camera. You explain the shot you have in mind and the presenter needs a couple of rehearsals to get the walk, words and timing right. You're getting stressed: 'Can't you just do it? The light's beginning to fade. You've had the script all day.'

At each stage of the production the presenter is getting the message that she's an afterthought, even though that isn't the message you want to put over. Ten minutes on the phone to brief her about the story before she left home would have given her a chance to prepare and might have produced some useful ideas for the programme (she is, after all, a professional travel writer). More sensitive handling on location would encourage a better performance. You might, for example, have reduced the stress and speeded up shooting by offering the use of 'idiot boards'(held up behind the camera showing the script or key phrases) or a large-print script taped below the lens.

The presenter is the public face of your programme. Looking after her needs benefits both of you: she is happier and you get a better performance.

Presenters and preparation for the studio

The studio is the place where the producer has control, almost complete control. Over sets, lighting, sound, props, inserts, interviews - and the presenter. Nothing happens in the studio unless the producer arranges for it to happen.

To exploit this control, you need detailed planning, far more detailed than is normally possible for location shoots.

This detail should extend to the role of the presenter. Where does he or she come in? Where does he stand or sit? Does he have any moves during the programme? Which camera does he talk to? Does he have autocue and, if so, on which camera? Does the design or colour of the set make it advisable to avoid certain clothes?

You should also give some thought to the presenter's role. It looks odd if he puts informed questions to a celebrity cook in one item and then in the next doesn't know how to boil an egg. Is he supposed to know about cooking, or isn't he?

The camera script (detailing camera numbers, positions and shot sizes) is a complicated document that goes through several drafts, usually before the presenter is available. Give him a copy as early as possible so that he can tailor the words to fit the way he speaks. Incorporate these changes into the script if they don't affect your shooting plans.

If you aren't using autocue and the presenter has to learn the script by heart, don't make last-minute changes yourself unless absolutely necessary.

You should pay for this preparation. If you pay for the studio day only, you shouldn't expect the presenter to do anything in advance beyond taking a phone call about programme contents and arrangements.

The studio day

Once again, however busy you are with rehearsals, don't forget the presenter. Make sure that he is kept accurately briefed and has research notes for any interviews. If at all possible, give him a chance to meet the interviewees before he sees them on the set. Once he has been introduced to interviewees, leave him alone with them so that they can bond. Interviewees often develop a good relationship with the producer or researcher who set up the interview. For a successful interview this relationship needs to be transferred to the presenter.

Give the presenter time to go to make-up. You should also let him view any prerecorded inserts before you go on air. If time is short, show him at least the first and last few shots so that he knows how to pitch the tone of his links. He also needs a chance to practise handling any props, particularly things like computers. If he can't get them to work on air, your programme is in trouble.

Don't call the presenter onto the studio floor until you are ready for him. Or ask him to wait around for ages while you are sorting out technical matters. It's tiring under the lights. Let him take a break and keep fresh for the recording.

When he arrives on the floor, give him time to check that the script on autocue is accurate and the position is right for his eyesight. Some presenters are short-sighted and don't like wearing glasses on air, so the position is important.

For dubbing with presenters see *In the dubbing theatre* on page 116.

Editing factual programmes

To avoid repetition I won't go over the points covered in *Editing basics* on page 34 and *Editing drama* on page 76. For the complete picture on editing factual programmes you need to refer to those sections too.

If you edit a factual programme in the same way that you edit a drama, you won't go far wrong. Surprise, tension, starting at the heart of the story and not the start - all these elements are as welcome in documentary as they are in drama.

But there are two big differences. In drama, the script is the starting point for putting the story together. With factual programmes, however, the closest thing to a script - the treatment - is not a good blueprint for editing. This is because storylines in most factual programmes are looser than in drama, and you are therefore less restricted in how you use the material to tell the story.

So when you view your factual material with the editor, be as objective as possible. Don't let the treatment or events on the shoot cloud your judgement. Look at what's on the screen and let that dictate how to put the programme together.

Interviews are the other thing that make drama different from factual editing. When you are viewing interviews, choose the chunks from which the final sound bites will come and put them in your first assembly. Don't bother about jump cuts between the sections at this stage.

When you've finished the first assembly and have viewed it the whole way through, you'll quickly realise which bits of interviews to drop and which to keep.

After a couple more viewings and re-edits, when you are down to the final sound bites, most of the jump cuts will probably have disappeared. You may decide to keep the remaining ones, if that's your style. Or cover them with a cutaway or carefully chosen shot illustrating what the interviewee is talking about.

Procedure for editing factual programmes

1   View and make a shot list, marking the best takes. Note chunks of interviews that contain possible sound bites.

2   Then make a list of usable sequences, shots and interviews in the order you would like to try for the first assembly.

3   Working fast with the editor, throw together a loose first assembly that lets you see the shape of the programme. If it's not right, you can change it. Better to get the shape right before you spend time on the details.

4   Don't worry if the first assembly is too long. It should be. Decide what's working and what can be made to work. Drop the rest.

5   Review the order of sequences. Is there a better opening than the one you have? Don't be frightened to experiment.

6   Remember the striptease principle: don't reveal more than necessary at that point in the story. If you keep viewers (and voyeurs) wanting more, they keep watching.

7   You're now ready to start fine-cutting: dropping shots that don't take the action forward, changing their order, finding better alternatives, trimming frames from their tops and tails to make cuts work as well as possible, and so on. Be painstaking on the fine cut. It's likely to be the stage that takes the most time.

8   Fine-cut sound too. Trim unwanted noise where you can and replace with wild track. Stagger sound and picture cuts so that they don't come at exactly the same moment: this makes the transition smoother. Add music and effects. Discuss with the editor which music might be best and take steps to acquire it. Remember copyright - see *Music and copyright* on page 73.

9   If you have the time and money, it's worth taking your film to a dubbing suite. There are three reasons. The dubbing suite is the only place in the production process where sound is the first and only priority. Your film also receives the attention of a specialist sound expert. And a well-mixed and well-balanced sound track will be best equipped to survive the assortment of delivery systems it will be subjected to during its lifetime.

10   If your programme may be sold abroad, don't forget to keep a separate copy of the M & E track (which includes Music, (sound) Effects and dialogue but not commentary) so that buyers can add a commentary in their own language.

Other points

1   Stay in the edit suite while the editor is working (observing and guiding, rather than instructing). It's the best place to learn how films are put together and - by extension - how to direct.

2   Think ahead. While the editor is working, start jotting down phrases and sentences for the voice-over commentary.

3   Decide what you want for graphics. If the requirements are simple and you have access to a suitable computer program, you could do them yourself. But don't overestimate your talents as a graphics designer. It's usually better to discuss what you need with a good designer and follow up regularly to check on progress.

4   Many people find that editing is the most rewarding and creative part of programme-making (I think so too). But factual programmes can be particularly difficult to edit. The process eats up time, if you want to end up with a polished programme. So expect long, hard hours in the edit suite.

REAL TIME

EDIT SUITE TIME

Graphics

If you know what you want and have time, there is no reason why you shouldn't use a computer program to do your own graphics (titles, credits, names, diagrams, maps and graphs). They don't have to be complicated: the simpler the better.

Take an analytical and critical look at graphics in other programmes and commercials. Do they work for you? Why? Are the ideas adaptable for your own programme?

Look also at ads and articles in newspapers and magazines. Printed ads have a fundamental advantage: people can look at a printed page as long as they like. TV commercials, however, can't linger indefinitely on the screen. So TV graphics have to go straight to the point. They can't be complicated.

Maps and diagrams

1   Good maps and diagrams give the minimum information. But it's the information you need: the London Underground map, for example, shows stations, lines, interchange stations, some sense of location. But it gives little sense of distance. Good maps leave out information you don't need.

2   TV maps have to be even more focused. If you want to show where something is, for example, ration yourself to a maximum of three names and a geographical feature (like a coast or river or mountain).

3   Keep graphs simple. They look like maths and frighten many viewers - 'I was no good at maths...' Label the axes clearly and underline the point of the graph in the commentary.

4   If you are comparing two or more variables, dramatise the relationship. Show the first, then superimpose the second, the third and so on.

5   Even better, if the content is suitable, animate your graphics. Remember: movement catches the eye.

6   Some colours (red, orange, yellow) are more eye-catching than others (dark browns and greens). Use colours to highlight significance.

7   Graphics should be beautiful as well as effective.

Words on screen

1   Use as few words as possible. Weed out the unnecessary.

2   Words, phrases and names don't need full stops or "inverted commas". Is any other punctuation really needed?

3   Select a font that's quick and easy to read. The smaller the font size, the harder it is to read. So err towards the large.

4   Choose colour, upper or lower case, alignment and other attributes to improve readability, not just to look nice.

5   Are words in the right part of the screen? Do they clash with faces or other key parts of the picture?

6   Don't put too many words on one screen. If the words are read out, viewers always read ahead. This weakens the punch line at the end. Save it for the next screen.

7   If words aren't read out, viewers read more slowly. Remember, viewers react more slowly than you do. They also don't know what is coming. So keep words on screen long enough to read aloud three times. This will give the right duration for viewers relaxing at home.

8   Arrivals and departures: how will words enter and exit screen? Cut, mix, wipe, scroll up or down, from left or right?

9   Remember cut-off. See page 51.

10   If you are putting graphics over shots, would adding a background or shadows or edging help visibility?

11   If the graphics aren't over shots, will the background be a photo, painting, pattern or..? Will the words be easy to read on the background?

12   When you have finished graphics, always ask a fresh pair of eyes to check them. Particularly the spelling. It's amazingly easy not to see mistakes - like a recent peak-time news item about the National Health Service entitled A HEALTY SERVICE?

Writing commentary

The key ideas for writing commentary (or voice-over or narration) are *write as you speak* and *write to picture*.

Write as you speak

Commentary is heard, not read. So use spoken language. The writing is merely a way of recording what you want to say - it's the means, not the end. Many people prefer to dictate commentary into a mini recorder. At the very least you should say it out loud before writing it down.

Spoken language is easier to understand than written language. This is important, as viewers have to absorb pictures at the same time as words. If the language is at all dense or difficult - long sentences with inherently complicated structures, formal, polysyllabic vocabulary, foggy statements full of qualifications and, of course, an habitual tendency to include lots and lots and lots of redundant words - viewers find they have forgotten the beginning of the sentence by the time the narrator has got to the end. Just as you have forgotten the beginning of the previous sentence. But you can read the sentence again. Viewers can't.

Writing spoken language can be difficult because it runs counter to what you may have been taught at school and university. To write as you speak, you should:

1   Use short words rather than long.
2   Use verbs rather than nouns (*the plan failed* is better than *the plan did not meet with success*).
3   Drop unnecessary words.
4   Drop adjectives and adverbs whenever possible.
5   Make simple, direct statements. Don't qualify them unless you have to.
6   Keep sentences short.
7   Include some very short sentences - maximum, 3-4 words.
8   Remember not all sentences need a verb. Really.
9   Avoid complicated sentence structures that are difficult to understand first time.
10 Recognise that sentences don't have to be linked, as in: *because it was raining, he stayed at home*. In narration, your thoughts reach viewers in sequence. Viewers expect them to be related. So write instead: *It was raining. He stayed at home.*

11 Avoid *the former...the latter*. Viewers won't remember what *the former* was. *Respectively* can cause similar problems.

12 Avoid including too many dates and facts in commentary (any more than you would in conversation). People won't remember them.

13 Distinguish between *which* and *that*. *Which* describes, *that* defines. *This is the house that Jack built* defines the house. *This is the house, which is green* describes the house. For some reason, people substitute *which* for *that* when writing. Use *that* in commentary, when appropriate. It works faster than *which*.

14 Avoid the posh. *Amidst, amongst, prior to, whilst* are all examples of posh. You rarely say them. Why write them?

15 Write simply. Unstuffy, everyday language has the widest appeal. This doesn't mean you should use slang, which may be incomprehensible outside a particular age group, profession or region.

Write to picture

To write to picture you have to edit the pictures first, then add the commentary. If you write the commentary first - you are making a word-led programme, with the drawbacks described in the *Introduction* (page 11).

It makes sense to edit the pictures first because pictures are more difficult to edit. They need a specific time to work on screen (you find out how long in the cutting room).

Words are easier to edit. They all work at roughly the same speed and you can add or lose or swap a few around to fit the picture without damaging the meaning. In fact, fitting words to pictures helps your writing. There usually aren't enough pictures to cover everything you want to say, so you have to make your writing short and sharp.

Write to picture, but don't describe the picture. One way to avoid this trap is to stand next to the screen and address your commentary to an imaginary viewer. Standing there, you quickly realise how daft it is to describe something your viewer can also see.

You also realise you don't need phrases like *This picture shows...* or *As you can see...* Viewers assume that the words refer to the pictures. You don't have to keep reminding them.

When you are writing, try to keep the link between verbal and visual as close as possible. Often a simple change in word order is enough. You might, for example, turn a sentence round so that a person isn't named before he appears on screen: *To get the volunteers out of bed, the university had to recruit a motivational expert, Doug Daily* (Doug Daily pops up on screen). The closer the link between name and person, the better.

Many pictures need no words because of the context, or because they show things happening. Others will need a few words to provide the *where? how? when?* and *why?* that the story needs. The words and pictures tell the same story, but each is telling a different part of the story.

Is a picture worth a thousand words?

If only the saying were always true. Pictures would speak for themselves and we would never have to write commentary. We also wouldn't have to add captions to photographs, or put labels next to paintings in art galleries.

For some types of information (the details of a face, for example) a picture is worth a thousand words. For other types (telling us who the person is) pictures are hopeless. (Where is the dividing line between the types of information? I don't know. If anyone does, I would love to hear from them.)

So another way of approaching commentary is to think of it as a way of filling in the information the pictures don't provide. What do viewers need to know that they can't see in the picture? That's what needs to go into the commentary.

Well-written captions in newspapers and magazines perform the same fill-in function. Captions are commentary writing for stills. They are worth studying if you want to write for TV.

Writers new to television

If a writer from another genre or a journalist is doing the commentary, don't assume that he or she knows how to do it, even if he has a shelf full of books to his credit. Commentary writing is a different craft.

Show them this section of the book. And check his words with the pictures at least a day before you go into the dubbing theatre. It will probably be brilliant. But it might need more work.

How to write commentary

1 Think about commentary and make notes while planning, shooting and editing

The thing to avoid is to find yourself facing an empty computer screen or blank sheet of paper on the night before the dub, when you can't put off writing any longer. Instead, you should let the commentary grow with the programme so that when you come to write it, you have a list of points to make, a few sections that are already complete and detailed notes for the rest.

Writing then becomes editing and polishing, rather than a search for inspiration.

2 Analyse shots and sequences

If you haven't already done so, take a step back from the programme and decide which shots need commentary and which shots don't. Writing 'wall to wall' (covering every shot between sound bites with words) is not the objective. Nonstop words are tiring for viewers. Pictures need to breathe and viewers need to get their breath back. So

- leave key parts of shots clear (usually when things are happening).
- avoid writing over close-ups, particularly of people talking.
- don't write over loud noises (e.g. explosions) or mood-creating sound effects (e.g. seagulls, dogs barking).

3 Writing to a recording

Most people like to write in front of a recording of the edited programme, trying out the lines as they go. This is convenient, but don't do it in the edit suite, where the editor could be getting on with other work. There is also the danger that you will spend ages fiddling with the controls and running shots over and over again instead of writing. As all writers know - any excuse for postponing work will do.

The other danger is that you speak faster when trying out lines on your own. When you are in the dubbing theatre, doing it for real, you are less relaxed, speak more deliberately and more slowly. So commentary that works when you are alone is often overlong in the dubbing theatre.

4   Listing commentary sections

You may find it faster and easier to write away from the edited programme. To do this you need a list of the sections that need commentary, and a layout (shown opposite) that makes it easy to count words.

For each section you need to write down the duration, a couple of words to remind you what's in the pictures, and the precise timing of anything your words should hit or avoid.

Also make a note of the opening and closing words of each sound bite.

5   Planning commentary

The next step is to jot down the points you want to make in each section. This gives you a feel for the relationship between commentary and pictures. It may highlight, for example, that you haven't a hope of making five points in the eight seconds leading up to a particular sound bite.

Leave the first and last two seconds of your story free of commentary. Viewers need time to take in the opening shot and vision mixers need time to cut away from the programme at the end.

Think carefully about where to start commentary. Delaying the start can be effective.

At the start of a commentary, you often need to tell viewers what they're looking at (*Shanghai, 1941*). You are then free to talk about things they can't see in the picture, like threats of war, corruption or imperialism. If viewers don't know what they are looking at, they will miss a lot of what you're saying because they don't understand the relevance of the pictures.

When you have finished your planning, ask yourself some questions:

- In sections where time is tight, which points are crucial?
- Would some points work better elsewhere? Would delay heighten interest? Provide information when it's needed and not before.
- Have you kept a good thought for the end? You need something that wraps up the story neatly or makes people think (a 'thumb sucker', as some people call it). Avoid the cliché ending: *Only time will tell.*

6 Layout

Allow two to three words for each second of picture; the exact number depends on the narrator and programme style. To simplify counting, reduce the margins on your computer to allow about six words per line. You then know that every line is two seconds long.

Start each chunk of commentary (known as a cue, or Q) with its timing - e.g. 4' 23". Within cues, write also the timing for key points that the commentary must hit exactly. Also the timing for the end of a cue, if it's followed by a sound bite and must not overrun. These extra timings in the script are helpful if you have to adjust the commentary during the dub.

You can add a refinement to this...

Timing	Shot	Commentary
03:00	MS James at PC	layout by marking out a time
2		line on the left of the page.
4		Then plot in the shots accord-
6		ing to their duration. If you've
8		allowed six words for a two-
03:10	CU script	second line, the words fill the
2		spaces next to the shots. You
4		don't have to count and can
6		instantly see if the commentary
8		fits just by looking at it. (3.20)
03:20	Interview (3.20)	"I thought of this layout...
		...a lot of trouble" (3:47)
03:47	Laying crazy paving	In crazy paving
03:~		the slabs are made ~ fit the

When checking timings, allow for pauses, emphases and dates. Write out dates as words (*nineteen eighty-four*). Written as numbers (*1984*), they look like only one word.

If a cue doesn't fit on a page, start a new page. This saves a turn-over in midsentence, and possibly a paper rustle.

Finally, however you lay out your pages, don't use tabs instead of margins. The computer treats tabs like words. Adding or dropping a word or tab makes the formatting go haywire.

7   **Write**

- Write as little as possible. Commentary is not a stand-alone essay. Words should support the pictures, not replace them.
- Keep commentary simple. If you find yourself using words like *paradox* or *antecedent*, your writing is too complicated.
- Don't worry if your words seem too straightforward. The pictures will add meaning, just as music adds meaning to lyrics.
- Try writing fast and then editing what you have written. Improving something you wrote quickly is often easier than getting it right in the first place.
- Don't forget that viewers won't read your commentary. They will hear it. So don't worry if lines look weak on the page, as long as they work with the picture. Some lines may read well, but are overwritten for the picture.
- Viewers can't hear quotation marks. A slight pause or a voice change is usually enough to signal a quote. But if the quote is just a couple of words, you probably need a phrase like *...as X called it.*
- Don't try and be funny, unless you are really good at it.
- Irony and sarcasm rarely work in commentary. Most viewers won't realise you're pulling their leg. Unless, of course, the writer is famous for his or her dry wit.
- Follow the points in *Write as you speak* on page 108.

8   **If stuck**

There will be times when the words don't come. Don't sit blankly before the screen or fiddle with the controls (computer or TV). There are better strategies.

- Look at the picture again. Why is it in the programme? The answer may not be linked directly to its content but may have more to do with the following shot.
- Don't think silent thoughts - say ideas out loud. Let yours ears decide. If it sounds right, it usually is right.
- Still working aloud, try talking someone through the pictures. Tell your listener what each section is trying to say. Why are the pictures there?
- Go on to the next section. Your subconscious will come up with answers while you are doing or thinking about something else.
- Get yourself a coffee or take a walk. Answers will pop up while you are on your way to the kettle or café or park.

9   Revise, revise, revise

- Read each section out loud to make sure you are using spoken language. You will hear where the words are wrong.
- Whenever you hear a fine but wordy phrase, ask yourself: would I say this to someone face-to-face? Does this sound like me? If not, rewrite, using simpler and more straight-forward language.
- Notice where you stumble or have to read sentences again. The problem is more often in the writing than the reading. Make changes to fix the problem.
- Look at every adjective and adverb. Would the line be stronger without it?
- Check again to see if you have written any short sentences: 3 to 4 words. If you haven't, can you introduce any?
- Are you saying things well? Can you make your points more neatly, precisely, powerfully?
- Have you avoided meaningless waffle? Price estimates of office blocks or earthquake damage; politicians *bracing themselves* for some development; policemen opening *incident rooms* to deal with a serious crime (so what?) - all these are fillers, containing little useful information. You would never say them to anyone face-to-face. Why use them on TV?

10   Check against the pictures

Read your words out against the pictures - slowly, as if you were in front of a mic Or it might be worth doing a dummy recording, using a computer or dictaphone.

If there are too many words for a section, don't assume that talking faster will get over the problem. Drop a few words.

Watch out also for awkward combinations of words and picture. A comment about a celebrity's popularity with the opposite sex might coincide with a shot of a potential partner. Embarrassment all round (possibly legal).

11   KISS and ABC

- Keep It Simple.
- Be Accurate, Brief, Clear.

12   Finally

Don't worry if you struggle. Commentary writing is difficult and can take a long time.

In the dubbing theatre

Choosing a voice

If a reporter or presenter appears on screen in the programme, it's normal for him or her to read the commentary or voice-over as well.

If you are going to hire a voice, choose carefully. Actors make excellent commentary readers, provided they don't act their socks off. An actor with a caring voice doesn't have to display epic emotion when narrating a programme about sick children. Restraint may be far more effective.

This poses the question: if you want restraint, why are you hiring an actor? There are lots of good reasons why you should (quality of voice, intonation, phrasing, publicity value etc.) but be clear what they are, before you pick up the phone.

You need to book (and pay) the chosen voice for long enough to do a good job. He or she needs to view the programme in advance and have time to try out the commentary against the pictures. Even with this preparation it can take up to two hours in the dubbing theatre to record commentary for a 50-minute programme (depending, of course, on how much commentary there is).

Preparation

If possible, send the narrator the script and a copy of the edited programme a day or two before the dub. If this isn't possible, ask him or her to come in early on the day of the dub. Let him read the script before viewing the programme.

Some parts of a script may make little sense without the pictures. (Some purists even maintain that this is the test of a well-written script. Maybe.) The narrator will notice these parts on his first read-through. He will then be looking out for the pictures that make sense of the words to inform his reading. For example: the emphasis on *port* in the sentence *Hong Kong is the third largest container port* will be weaker if you can see the port.

In the same way a narrator will say a word or phrase quite differently if he knows that the word or phrase is setting up (or picking up) something said in an interview.

This preparation also gives the narrator a chance of altering the script to suit his or her own speech rhythms. How many changes should you allow? Obviously a complete rewrite is out of the question. If the narrator finds that he is so out of sympathy with the script that only a rewrite will do, then you're probably better off finding another narrator. (If this happens, get a second opinion on the script. Narrators don't turn down a fee lightly. Perhaps the script *is* dire.)

Minor changes, however, are acceptable, provided they don't affect the fit with the pictures. Acceptable also are changes designed to avoid injudicious juxtapositions (try saying that aloud).

If you have time, get the narrator to do an out-loud read-through with the pictures. This saves time in the dubbing theatre, always a good idea. Dubbing theatres cost more than viewing machines.

Before this read-through discuss with the narrator the approach you have in mind: 'relaxed and chatty' or 'businesslike and matter-of-fact' or 'not too emotional'.

In the cubicle

Introduce the narrator to the mixer (the person who operates the dubbing equipment) and then take the narrator to the cubicle.

Some narrators like to stand up while reading. Fine. If they prefer to sit, check that the chair and the mic are at the right heights and put the script on a lectern, so that the narrator doesn't have to look up to see the monitor and cue light.

The narrator should have the screen in peripheral vision but discourage him or her from taking his own cues from the screen. Only a few experienced professionals can do it successfully. Even they have problems if there's a read-on (when one cue runs over into the next).

There's also a decision to be made about the headphones or 'cans'. Does the narrator want to hear his own voice (feedback), or just the effects (FX) on the film? Leave this decision to the narrator. Experienced voices usually prefer to hear their own voices and FX; less experienced ones are better off with FX only.

Finally, ask him or her to remove any staples from the script. This minimises the rustling when he turns to the next page.

Recording

Go back to the main part of the dubbing theatre and ask the narrator to start reading the first few sections of commentary. This gives the dubbing mixer a chance to adjust the level to suit the narrator's voice.

When mixer and narrator are happy, ask the mixer to start the recording procedure. He or she will alert the narrator by saying 'We're running' or 'Stand by'. At the appropriate moment you need to press the cue button to start the narrator reading. It's quite an art to get the timing right. You should give the cue anything from one third to two thirds of a second early so that the narrator has a moment to react.

You may prefer to delegate cueing to the mixer so that you can concentrate on getting the best possible reading. Keep an ear open for 'fluffs' (minor mistakes, hesitations, stutters). Think about the way the narrator is reading: would a different approach to a sentence or phrase produce a better result? Are the speed and emphases right? Are the words hitting the right pictures?

If something goes wrong or you spot a possible improvement, don't be too quick to stop the recording. Ignore the occasional fluff - you can rerecord and drop in a correction later. Ignore also near misses of word and picture - the sound can be moved back or forwards later to improve the fit. The advantage of fewer stops is that you don't break the narrator's flow. The downside is the time it takes to patch things up later.

If the narrator stumbles or stutters, remember it's almost always the fault of the writing. Despite your checks, some tongue twisters get through, like *the new business's assets were seized* or *crumb-crisp coating* (the latter phrase made Orson Welles blow his top when he was asked to read it in a commercial). The narrator may be able to get round the problem. But it's better to fix the writing. If there are too many words, drop a few rather than ask the narrator to read faster. Shorter is better.

If there's a problem with an emphasis or a part of the delivery, explain the problem and maybe suggest a way round it, like 'This refers to the earlier line about his hopes'. Don't read out passages for the narrator to copy.

As ever, be generous with words of approval. Compliment when you can.

Inexperienced narrators

Sometimes a person who is not used to narrating or performing has problems projecting his or her voice: he sounds like he is talking to himself. There are various ways you can help.

- Suggest the reader imagines someone behind the microphone and talks to them instead of the mic The someone might be a partner or teenager or boss (note the choice of person can colour the tone of voice).

- A chronically shy voice can sometimes be coaxed into an acceptable recording by being asked to ham it up wildly. His or her idea of hamming it up wildly may be closer to your idea of a normal delivery.

- Sometimes the failure to project the voice (usually the result of nerves) takes over only when you start to record. If you suspect that this may happen, record the rehearsal without telling the narrator.

- Narrators often find it easier to project their voices when standing. Or when they wave their arms about. Tell them not to be shy. Wave away. No-one's watching.

A good dub can transform your programme

A good dub can add another layer of meaning to your programme. A bad dub can badly weaken it. So don't treat the dub as a tiresome chore. Move commentary lines earlier or later to get their position in relation to the pictures precisely right. Add music and sound effects where appropriate and make sure the levels of commentary, music and sound effects don't fight.

Ask the mixer if you can check the results on a standard TV speaker rather than the expensive, high quality speakers used for dubbing. The professional equipment there often gives a misleading impression of what people will hear at home. Low level bass and high treble that sound great on big speakers may be inaudible on a standard domestic TV set.

Don't forget that the dubbing mixer has been through more dubs (good and bad) than you. Don't be frightened to ask his or her advice if you have a problem or want a second opinion.

Time and money

Sooner or later - usually sooner - you come up against the problem of money. How much will it cost?

The answer to 'How much?' depends on two 'How long?' questions. How long is the film going to be? How long will it take to make?

Let's say you are going to make a 10 minute film.

Time

To estimate production time you need some idea of the number of shots in the finished piece. Establish this by viewing programmes of the sort you are making and counting shots in a random sample of minutes. My samples came up with an average of 6 shots per minute. This gives a total of 60 shots for a 10 minute programme. Add 33% (20 shots) for close-ups, reaction shots etc. that you shoot for editing purposes. So you need 80 shots in all for your film.

This is the sum for 6-7 minutes per setup, 20 minutes for the first shot, 30 minutes for clearing up and 3 locations:

First shots: 20 min. x 3 locations	1h 00m
Clear-up time: 30 min. x 3 locations	1h 30m
77* shots x 6 min. per shot	7h 42m
Total shooting time	10h 12m

80 minus the first shot on 3 locations

You might think just over 10 hours is a long day's work. But add travel time, refreshment breaks, mishaps, weather, sound and light problems and it would be safer to allow for 2 days to shoot your film, especially if there is any lighting involved.

How do interviews affect these calculations? If your 10 minute film consists of a single talking head plus some illustrative material, you might be able to shoot it in one day. But if there are four or five talking heads, the interviews probably won't save any shooting time and will increase the editing time.

How long will the programme take to edit? You need to allow at least 3 x shooting time - 4 or more if the structure is complicated and there's lots of material. 3 x shooting time may appear too much, but it's a bit optimistic, if anything.

This becomes clear when you start thinking about shooting ratios. Say you shoot 100 minutes of material for a 10 minute film - a 10:1 shooting ratio. That seems generous. But divide your 100 minutes by 2 (the shooting days) and your 'allowance' for each day is only 50 minutes, less than two cassettes full. This seems a pitifully small bag for a hard day's work on location.

Let's double shooting productivity by assuming you shoot 4 x 30 minute cassettes every day - 8 cassettes in all, about 4 hours of material. It's going to take the best part of one editing day just to transfer the material into the edit machine, view and log it.

With 4 hours of material your shooting ratio has gone up to 24:1. Lose control of the ratio (30:1 is not unusual) and you are spending a lot of editing time on preliminaries. A way round this is to do some form of pre-edit by viewing and pruning the material before transferring it (see *Make a shot list* on page 76).

Money

If you have gone through the estimating procedure above, you will have some idea of what you need and how long you need it for. The next step is to ask potential suppliers what they will charge. Then fill in the list on the next two pages.

Some of the items (e.g. scriptwriter and commentary writer) are contradictory and unlikely to be needed in the same production. On the other hand, you may have to spend money on things that aren't included, like hairdressing, cleaning, animation, stunts, or special effects.

Note that if there are animals in your programme (furry or feathered, not just people you don't get on with) your stock costs may rise. Animals rarely perform on cue. You may also have to pay for special trainers or handlers. Similarly, if you are using children, you may have to pay for chaperones or teachers.

The final item (a 15% contingency fee) is a sensible precaution to allow for the fact that most things end up costing more than you expect. And to give you that warm feeling of success when you make a great programme and it ends up on budget - or even a little under.

	Man days	Days x rate	Expenses	Total
People & Kit				
Producer				
Scriptwriter				
Director				
PA/secretary				
Researcher				
Performers rehearse				
Performers record				
Other contributors				
Cameraman + kit				
Sound man + kit				
Lighting man + kit				
Camera assistant				
Sound assistant				
Special equipment				
Set designer				
Set construction				
Props acquisition				
Props assistant				
Costume				
Make-up				
Safety				
Editor(s) + suite				
Commentary writer				
Dubbing				
PR/photographer				
Other				

	Man days	Days x rate	Expenses	Total
Materials				
Shooting stock				
Transfers				
Other cassettes				
Location fees				
Hire cars + parking				
Coffees/teas				
Catering				
Petty cash				
Titles and credits				
Rostrum				
Other graphics				
Archive film & stills				
Music/copyright				
Music composition				
Music recording				
Insurance				
Publicity				
Postage				
Hospitality				
Bank interest				
Launch party				
Competition entry				
Miscellaneous				
Total				
15% Contingency				
GRAND TOTAL				

Going Solo

Preliminaries

Going solo - operating the camera and directing at the same time - is not easy. To do a good job you have to be able to find your way round the essential controls on your camera without thinking.

Your camera may have a hundred or more buttons, switches and menus, but the four controls you have to master are those for zoom, focus, exposure and sound. *Going Solo* is designed to get you up to speed on these, as well as introduce you to some of the others. It offers a step-by-step introduction (with exercises) to the camera. It will also help you find your way round the camera manual.

Unpack the camera

Careful! Keep the packaging. You may need it if the camera has to be returned for repair or service.

Check that you have all the bits and pieces listed in the manual. Make sure you keep all the leaflets and cards to register for the guarantee. You'll need to send them off when you've given your machine the once-over.

Charge a battery

Consult the manual on how to do this. If at first you can't slide and click the battery into the charger or camera, don't force it. Take a closer look at the instructions and diagrams and try again. It should click in easily. If you have to force it, you're doing it wrong (a useful rule for everything you do with the camera).

Charging a battery may take two to five times longer than the recording time you get from the charged battery, so don't think of it as a quick turn-round operation.

Batteries discharge themselves over a period of time, so if you haven't used the camera for a while, you need to recharge. The best time to do this is the day or night before the shoot, particularly if you don't have a separate charger and have to use the camera itself for recharging.

If you have a charger and are doing a big shoot, take the charger on location so that you can recharge while you are shooting.

If it's the first time you have unpacked the camera and you are in a hurry to get going, you may be able to run it from the mains or from a car battery, using a transformer and cables (which often have to be bought separately). Don't be tempted to use batteries from another camera or manufacturer. The guarantee will only cover power packs listed in the manual.

Most camcorders have a symbol or figures in the viewfinder showing how much battery time is left. When the battery is about to run out completely, symbols start to flash. Don't rely on the time-remaining figure too much. It can't take into account your style of shooting (long continuous takes or lots of starting and stopping), whether you are using the viewfinder or foldout screen, how cold it is and how much zooming and auto-operation is going on - all these affect battery life. So don't take risks with the crucial shoots: use a fresh battery for interviews with Presidents and Prime Ministers.

Get into the habit of conserving batteries. Don't play back or rewind tapes in the camera unnecessarily (this also wears the heads unnecessarily). And always have a charged spare handy.

Battery care

Don't put spare batteries in a pocket or bag together with anything metal, like keys or coins. These may create a short circuit or discharge the battery or - even worse - start a fire. Also keep batteries dry and away from metal surfaces. Put them in a plastic bag or paper envelope if you are carrying them around.

Work out a way of differentiating charged and uncharged batteries. Some battery cases have a red spot with a sliding cover for doing this. Another way is to mark charged batteries with camera tape or a rubber band that you have to take off before you start using the battery. Also give them each a number so that you can spread the load by using them in rotation.

To extend overall battery life, avoid topping up. Most batteries benefit by being charged and discharged fully.

The information about batteries in the manual may be under several headings but look it up and read it. Without power your camera is dead.

Load the cassette

The first thing to do is fix a charged battery to the camera. Then take the cassette out of its case - not as straightforward as you might think. Some tops look like they should flick open - but don't. The trick is to dig a fingernail between the bottom and the back of the case and then lift the front upwards from the bottom.

Then make sure the sliding tab at the bottom of the cassette (the write-protect tab) is covering the hole - this is the record position. If the hole is open (the save position) or the red dot is showing or there's no tab, you won't be able to record on the tape. This is a safety feature to stop you recording over pictures you want to keep.

Next, find the eject button on the camera to activate the cradle that takes the cassette. The eject button may not work if the camera isn't switched on. If this is so, switch on and make sure the camera is in camera mode, not VCR (the playback and editing mode). If it isn't, press the mode button to swap to camera, which is what you want.

Which way should the cassette go into the cradle? Look inside the cradle and you will see twin cores that slot into the twin holes in the cassette. So the cassette holes need to be on the inside. At the bottom of the cradle (usually) you will also see the guides for the tape. The moveable flap on the cassette (which protects the tape) therefore goes in first. As a double-check, the write-protect tab should be facing upwards. If the orientation is wrong, the cassette won't drop fully into the cradle.

When the cassette is in the cradle, gently push the cradle or the button on the cradle lid. On some cameras you have to push the inner cradle first, then the outer lid. You should hear a whirring noise as the cassette is loaded.

Whenever you finish recording and eject a cassette, slide the write-protect tab to the save position so that you can't record over your material by mistake.

Then label the cassette so that you know what's on it. Avoid using private codes like ##. It won't mean anything to someone looking for a cassette in a hurry. They may just assume the cassette is blank and go ahead and use it.

Adjust the viewfinder

You have to switch the camera on before you can adjust the viewfinder.

Some viewfinders are fixed parts of the camera; others are tubes that you tilt up or down. Some tubes collapse like a telescope so that they pack away neatly.

Once you have extended the tube, you can focus the viewfinder by turning a thumb-wheel or sliding a tab until the letters and symbols on the viewfinder screen are sharp. On some cameras you can adjust the viewfinder brightness through the control menus.

These focus and brightness adjustments affect the viewfinder only; they won't make any difference to the pictures you record.

On some cameras you can slide the viewfinder sideways and fix it in the most convenient position with a locking screw; this lets you choose which eye to use. (Experienced cameramen develop the knack of keeping one eye on the viewfinder and watching the action with the other.)

If you can't see a picture on the screen, check the front of the lens to make sure you have removed the lens cap.

The viewfinder concentrates light, so direct sunlight falling on it may damage the display. As a general rule, it's not a good idea to leave your camera in the sun when it's not in use. If you do have to put it down, leave it in the shade and check that the viewfinder is turned away from the light.

Remember also that sun and shade move.

Adjust the monitor screen

The monitor screen is normally on the left of the camera. It should fold out till it's at right angles to the camera. Don't force it beyond that - you may break it. Check the manual to see how far it will open.

Have the screen facing down when you are holding the camera above your head, and up when the camera is near the ground.

The screen should be able to rotate vertically to face the front: useful when you are recording yourself in a video diary.

On some cameras you can click the monitor back into the side of the camera so that the screen is facing outwards. It continues to show video and audio in this position and the picture is still the right way up. Neat!

But remember that the monitor is comparatively fragile. Be careful not to let the camera roll over when the monitor is in the viewing position and never force it when rotating it. Also don't use it to pick up or hold the camera.

If you need to adjust the brightness and colour of the monitor screen, there may be some buttons next to it, or on its edges but you will probably have to go into the control menus.

You also need to familiarise yourself with how to navigate through the menu lists, select an item, set it and then exit back to the main menu.

Don't worry what all the headings mean: some are very technical, some work only if the camera is set to the right mode (camera or VCR) and there are many you will never use. Even so, be prepared to find your first encounter a bit scary.

Monitor screen

Advantages

- It's safer because your world is no longer confined to the shot. Your eye isn't glued to the viewfinder, so you can keep an eye on what is happening outside the shot.

- During interviews you can maintain eye contact with interviewees. They can talk to a real person instead of a lens.

- It's easier to frame high- and low-angle shots. If you swivel the screen forwards, the subject can see his or her own performance. Some people find this helpful, others less so.

- The monitor is ideal for viewing playback of a shot.

Drawbacks

- The monitor may give a misleading account of the colour and brightness of the picture you are recording, either because it is wrongly adjusted or because it is fighting the prevailing light.

- In bright sunlight it can be difficult to see much on the screen. You can try shading the screen or adjusting the brightness to improve the picture but it's faster and easier to go back to using the viewfinder.

- It's more difficult to hold the camera still when you are using the monitor than when you are using the viewfinder. Holding the viewfinder against your eye helps to steady the camera.

- The viewfinder is better for observing detail.

- The monitor uses more power than the viewfinder. If you need to conserve batteries, use the viewfinder.

SP or LP

Before you can start shooting you may have to choose a recording speed - standard (SP) or long play (LP). Stay with SP unless you have a good reason not to. LP (sometimes known as extended play, EP) makes the tape last 1½ to 2 times longer, but there's less information going onto the tape so the picture and sound quality will not be quite as good.

Try to avoid converting material from one speed to the other; conversions cost time and money. And, of course, it's not sensible to mix speeds on the same cassette.

Can your edit suite work with LP? Do you have a machine to play LP cassettes into the edit machine or will you have to use the camera (which may not be available) to play them in? Do you have the leads for linking camera and edit equipment?

Final checks

Make sure you understand the meaning of the symbols on the viewfinder and monitor screen.

Check that the main controls (focus, exposure, white balance) are on auto. Check also that the camera is set to 'Shoot' or 'Cam[era]' or 'Camcorder', not VCR.

You are now ready to shoot!

Press the shoot/start button. You should see REC(ord) or a flashing light on the monitor screen or viewfinder; a light on the front of the camera may also come on. (If you are doing undercover shooting or want to stop the light reflecting in a window, cover it up with tape or switch it off via the menus.)

Other signs that you are recording: you will hear a slight whirr from the motor as it pulls the tape across the heads. You may also be able to see the spools turning through a little window in the cradle (for undercover shooting, tape this up too).

These signs that the camera is recording are important. It's easy to start recording by mistake. Even professional cameramen have been known to think they were recording, then switched off and put the camera down, only to find that the camera was off when they thought it was running and vice versa. Result: missed action and a lengthy shot of the ground. Annoying. Get into the habit of checking that the camera is running when you think it's running - and has stopped when you stop it.

If nothing happens

If the camera doesn't start as it should, check the following.
- The batteries are correctly inserted.
- The mains cable isn't loose.
- You are in shoot or camera mode, not VCR.
- The sliding tab on the cassette is in the record position.

If these checks don't work, consult the manual.

Bars and tone

If your camera generates colour bars and tone (find out from the manual) and your transfer and editing equipment can use them, record bars and tone on the first 30 seconds of the cassette. These establish reference standards for picture and sound and are used to set up postproduction equipment.

Even if you don't record bars and tone, don't put anything you might want to use on the first 30 seconds of tape. There are often faults at the start of a tape and the transfer or editing machinery may need it for threading the tape past the heads.

Reviewing the recording

Most cameras have a review (or record-check) button that will rewind and show the last few seconds of the shot. Use this to check that pictures and sound are going onto the tape (you may need headphones for the sound). If your camera doesn't have a review button, you will have to use the VTR mode to check there's a recording.

You should do this record-check whenever you start a new cassette or have used the camera in VTR mode. But don't waste time by reviewing after every shot. If you have doubts about a shot, it's safer and quicker to reshoot.

Using camera standby

The camera will display STBY or PAUSE or an appropriate icon on the viewfinder screen when it is in standby or pause. The advantage of standby is that the camera will start recording immediately you press the button - you don't have to wait for the tape to lace up.

The disadvantage of standby is that the recording head spins round touching the tape. To stop it damaging the tape and to save the battery the camera will automatically switch off or go into save mode after about four or five minutes.

Point and shoot

Point and shoot is the most straightforward way to use the camcorder. You point the camera, zoom to the shot you want and press the record button. You don't have to worry about technical details: the camera looks after focus, exposure, white balance, sound and wobble.

In many situations this is fine: shots of the children in the garden, holiday shots on the beach, outings to the park and the zoo, group photos at birthdays, weddings, graduations and all the other rituals that are fun to capture on camera.

Point and shoot is also ideal when you are using the camera as a notebook and picture quality is not the most important consideration: for example, when you are house hunting and your partner or flatmate(s) can't come to the first viewing.

Point and shoot, however, is not ideal in all situations. It comes unstuck when conditions - or the pictures you want - are a bit unusual.

If you're shooting through a window, for example, autofocus will have a problem deciding whether to focus on the glass or the scene behind it. Or, if you're shooting a subject standing in front of a bright window, should the autoexposure expose for the subject or the scene outside the window? In these and other situations you can't be sure of first-class results using the auto systems. It's better to go manual.

Having said that, point and shoot is probably OK for 60-70% of the material you shoot. As you become more experienced and get to know the camera better, you'll know exactly when you can rely on auto and when you can't.

Exercises

- Charge a battery.
- Load a cassette.
- Adjust the monitor screen or viewfinder.
- Switch on and record something. Familiarise yourself with the lights and icons that tell you the camera is running.
- Pause or standby the camera. Check how the camera shows it's paused or on standby. Use the playback or review button to check you have recorded pictures and sound.

Explore the zoom

Essentials

The zoom is the fun feature on a camcorder. The moment anyone switches on a camera, they start playing with the zoom: in a bit, out a bit, in again, out. It's satisfying.

It's also natural, because the zoom reproduces in a crude sort of way what your eyes do. When you look at a scene, your eyes are drawn to something that is bright or moves. You might then take in the whole scene in long shot, flick to a close-up of something that interests you, flick back again to the thing that's moving, and so on. These changes of fixation are known as saccades and are a basic characteristic of how we see. So perhaps playing with the zoom reproduces the need to keep changing the view.

But there's a big difference between our eyes and the zoom. Our eyes switch instantly from shot to shot; the zoom takes time. Our eyes cut. The zoom zooms. The zooming part isn't natural; it's a means to an end, not the end itself. Unless the zooming is hidden or well motivated, it draws attention to itself.

You zoom in by pressing the T end of the control. T stands for telephoto: the narrow, telescope end of the lens. W stands for wide-angle. How long a zoom takes depends on the camera and your finger pressure on the control. Press harder for faster. Experiment to see how fast and how slow your zoom can go. Can the autofocus keep up when you zoom in fast?

The great advantage of the zoom is that it's brilliant for finding the best size for a shot. When you have set up a shot, get into the habit of zooming in a little closer to see if it improves the picture. You should do this when the camera is in pause or standby so that your efforts to find the best framing aren't recorded.

If you have started to record and then decide to improve the framing by a little zoom - don't. Your viewers won't thank you for the supposed improvement in the framing. They will, however, notice a tiny (and, as far as they are concerned, pointless) movement, however small it is. Fiddling with the framing while recording is just a bad habit.

When to zoom

So when do you use the zoom? Let's assume you want to start
with a wide shot of a street and then zoom in to a close-up of a
No Parking sign. Your eyes flick instantly between street and
sign and the viewer probably wants to do the same. This would
suggest cutting between the shots, but you want to do a zoom as
well. To keep both options open, put the camera on a tripod and
record the long shot for 8-10 seconds, then zoom in and hold the
close-up for 8-10 seconds. You can then decide in the edit if the
zoom or cutting between the static shots serves your purpose
better.

Zooms work best when they are **motivated** by the action in the
shot, or **combined** with another camera movement, or
progressively reveal content in a scene. Some examples:

- You zoom with a moving object, such as a car moving away
  from the camera.
- You zoom while you pan - for example, panning with a river
  steamer while zooming in to a close shot of the bows. (When
  you are close enough, stop panning and hold the shot steady
  while the steamer glides through the shot and exits.)
- You zoom out instead of in. In the street-to-no-parking
  example zooming-in is a dull way of emphasising something
  that's already in the shot. It doesn't show the viewer
  anything new. If, on the other hand, you zoom out from the
  No Parking sign to show that the street is jammed with cars
  ignoring the sign, the zoom makes a point.

How fast?

If you find a shot where you think a zoom will work, it's often difficult to know how fast or slow the zoom should be. If you're not sure, do it two or three times at different speeds. You can then choose the one that works best during the edit.

If you want a timed zoom, you can count seconds fairly accurately by saying 'One (thousand), two (thousand), three (thousand)...'

Extras

Manual zoom

Experiment with the manual control, a ring that wraps round the lens. Is the ring moving the lens or is it controlling a motor that does the work (like power steering in a car)?

If the zoom is powered, it will have built-in quirks designed to smoothen jerky hand moves. You will find that it has a delayed reaction to sudden starts and stops, and it may not respond at all if you move the ring very slowly. You can also keep on turning the ring after you've reached the end of the lens (an odd feeling, this).

Does the ring allow you to do a crash zoom (a zoom at maximum speed)? How well does the autofocus keep up with a fast or crash zoom?

The best manual zooms have a little bar sticking out at right angles to the zoom ring. Holding the bar you can zoom up or down the entire range of the lens in one action without changing your grip. This may be difficult or impossible to do if you have to grip the zoom ring.

A manual zoom makes no noise. This is an important advantage for some cameras, where the on-board microphone is next to the lens and picks up the whirring of the zoom motor. If you want to zoom while recording sound on these cameras, you have to go manual.

What are the disadvantages of a manual zoom? It may be more difficult to keep the zooming movement steady. But your technique will improve with practice.

Digital zooms

Camcorders are becoming more and more like telescopes, with some camcorders boasting magnification multiples of 600 or more. On such cameras the close and middle parts of the range are produced optically, by changing the position of the lenses inside the barrel. But the telephoto part of the range, where the magnification is greatest, is produced electronically, which means that the camera mimics the zooming effect by taking a smaller and smaller part of the picture and magnifying it.

This magnification is achieved by distributing the pixels for the chosen area across the whole screen and then repeating pixels to fill in the gaps. So the digital zoom doesn't capture any extra detail - it simply spreads the information more thinly.

As the magnification increases, the picture quality gets worse and it begins to look like a photocopy of a photocopy of a photocopy... The depth of field shrinks and focus becomes more difficult to find. It also becomes impossible to hold the shot steady without a tripod. Other factors such as air pollution and heat shimmer - which you don't normally have to worry about - can also become significant at such high levels of magnification.

So it would be a mistake to buy a camera just because it has a powerful zoom. The digital end of the lens may indeed be capable of ferocious close-ups, like filling screen with an envelope on the other side of the street. But - be honest - how often do you want to shoot something as extreme as this?

If you want a big close-up of something small and can get the camera close to the subject, you will get a better picture with more apparent depth by zooming out and moving the camera in so close that it almost touches the subject. If there is enough light you'll find the minimum focus distance is almost zero.

All the above doesn't mean the extreme end of the zoom is useless. I'm just pointing out that it's not the answer to all your prayers. Sometimes it does offer an answer, making possible, for example, startling close-ups of birdnests on unclimbable cliffs.

Macro
On many cameras the digital zoom has supplanted the macro. But your camera may have a macro (either built-in or as a separate attachment), offering extreme close-ups when the camera is very close to the subject. This lets you fill the screen with something as small as a detail on a postage stamp. The depth of field (the area in focus) is very narrow, so you have to focus carefully and settle for the background being out of focus (though this can be attractive).

Exercises

- Practise using the power and the manual zoom on:
    a static target such as a notice board
    a moving target such as a duck swimming on a lake
- How smooth are the zooms? How necessary is the tripod? Try varying the speed of the zooms.

- Practise crash zooms (as fast as you can go) using both power and manual zooms.

- Set up a shot which lets you zoom from a foreground to a background subject and vice versa. How close to the foreground object can you move the camera without losing focus? Try seeing how close you can move the camera with the lens zoomed in and zoomed out.

- Play with the telephoto end of the digital zoom. It's a great snooping device. How can you use it in a programme?

Explore focus

Essentials

Most cameras will offer three ways of focusing - **auto**, **manual** and **push focus**.

Autofocus

You simply point the camera and the auto adjusts the focus for you. This works fine in many situations, depending on the speed and sophistication of the device on your camera.

When the autofocus is switched on, you will see a little icon in the viewfinder. If you don't know which the focus icon is, consult the manual or find the autofocus control and switch it on and off to see what changes. With the autofocus switched off, there's usually a hand or a 'M' next to the focus icon to show that you are on manual.

Manual focus

To change to manual focus, press the manual adjust buttons or rotate the focus ring round the lens. These controls may override the autofocus switch. If they don't, you will have to switch autofocus off before operating the manual ring or buttons.

Once you are on manual, you can fiddle with the control until the focus is sharp.

There is, however, a far better technique: zoom in to the part of the picture you want in sharp focus (usually the subject's eyes) and adjust the control until the picture is sharp. Then zoom out again to the size of shot you're after. This works because the depth of field (the area of the picture in focus) is at its narrowest at the narrow end of the zoom (when you are zoomed in).

Once the focus is sharp at maximum close-up, it is sharp for all sizes of shot, provided the distance between camera and subject stays the same. You can now select any size of shot and even zoom in and out to your heart's content without losing focus.

Push focus

When you are zoomed in, you can find the correct focus using the manual ring or buttons, but in fact it's quicker and easier to use the push-focus button (not all cameras have one). This switches the lens to auto, finds focus and then switches back to manual.

Focusing on the move

If you are following children round a funfair or grabbing shots of someone showing off their favourite plants in the garden, reframing and refocusing for each bit of the action takes too long and breaks up the flow of the action.

In these situations the easiest way to keep things in focus is to zoom out to a wide shot (the wider the shot, the wider the depth of field) and keep the camera close to the subjects. This technique minimises wobbles and keeps the subjects dominant in the picture, so that viewers feel they are right in there with the action.

Extras

Use the manual focus

When the focus changes rapidly Focus adjustments (auto or manual) during a shot are not pretty and destroy the illusion you are creating. The autofocus won't hold steady, for example, if a passer-by walks through the shot close to the camera. And if you do a shot driving down a street with some houses near the pavement and some set back, the shot will show more focusing than focus.

When there is a choice of subject to focus on This usually happens if the point of interest is not in the centre of the frame or occupies only a small part of the picture. The autofocus may rock between the various points of interest, hunting for focus. This may also happen if you are filming something through glass or barbed wire or garden railings or a net.

When there's nothing stable or distinct to focus on A field of swaying wheat, for example. Or when you are shooting in low light and everything is grey and there isn't much contrast. Most autofocus systems work by detecting sharp edges. These are less distinct in low-contrast scenes.

Throw or pull focus

A sudden focus change from foreground to background or vice versa can be a dramatic way of showing new information. For the effect to work you need narrow depth of field and two objects that are at significantly different distances from the camera.

Take depth of field first. In bright light when the aperture is smaller (the higher f-numbers) the depth of field may be so great that it is impossible to throw focus. Try introducing an ND filter. This reduces the light going into the camera and lets you increase the aperture one or two f-numbers. The wider open the aperture, the narrower the depth of field. You may now be able to throw focus where previously you couldn't.

If it's still impossible to throw focus, try moving the camera closer to the foreground object. Throw focus won't work if the foreground and background objects are close to each other and both are some distance away from the camera. If you move the camera closer to the foreground object, the background object is relatively much further away. With luck it will be beyond the reach of the foreground area of focus.

Exercises

- With the autofocus on, zoom out to wide-angle. Everything more than about a metre away should be in focus.
- Pan the camera from something nearby to something distant. Watch the autofocus adjust. How fast does it do this? How smooth is the adjustment if you pan slowly?
- Now zoom in to the narrow end and pan the camera. Watch the autofocus adjust when the depth of field is narrow. Notice how this end of the lens exaggerates wobbles.
- Now zoom out and alter the proportions of the picture taken by foreground and background subjects until you find the point where the autofocus rocks between the two. This is because it doesn't know which subject to focus on. You may have to move the camera to find the rocking point.
- Practise throwing focus manually.
- Find out if the autofocus can keep up with the zoom. Does it have to catch up when you zoom in fast?

Explore exposure

Essentials

The autoexposure, AE for short, controls the amount of light entering the camera by adjusting the size of the aperture and, in some circumstances, the shutter. It also controls the gain feature, which electronically amplifies low light.

The most common use is adjusting the size of the aperture or iris (the opening behind the lens that lets the light in). Aperture sizes are defined by f-numbers. The bigger the number (f16, or f22 on some lenses), the smaller the aperture.

The autoexposure will always try to find a balance between the bright and dark parts of the picture, showing as much detail as possible in both. In even light, when there's not too much contrast between bright and dark, the autoexposure will give good pictures. It may not be as successful when there is **too little light**, **too much light**, **strongly contrasting light** and **light that moves**.

Too little light

Camcorders have an impressive ability to lighten up dark scenes. Overcast days look much brighter on the screen than they do in real life. In dark and gloomy locations the auto-exposure may switch itself on and bring into play the electronic feature known as gain, which is a sort of volume switch for light, adjusting the brightness in 3dB steps to a maximum of 18 dB (dB, short for decibel, is better known for measuring sound levels).

The higher the dB, the more the camera brightens the scene. The drawback is that as gain increases, picture quality deteriorates. You may prefer to switch to manual exposure and reduce the gain a little, thus trading off a little brightness against a less grainy picture.

If you want gloom or shade to be dark on screen (say, inside a church) you have to set the exposure to manual - auto will make it brighter. Many cameras offer a preset exposure (program AE) to record gloom but the result may not be what you have in mind.

Too much light

The camera may record unsatisfactory pictures in very bright daylight even when the exposure is reduced to f16 or the minimum. If you switch to manual exposure, you may be able to go beyond the minimum and close the aperture completely - interesting, but not much use for shooting.

A better solution for very bright light is to use the neutral density (ND) filter. Your camera may have two strengths of filter and automatically indicate which should be used. ND filters work like sunglasses, evenly reducing all the light entering the camera but not affecting the colours.

Strongly contrasting light

Most cameras can cope with contrast (the ratio between the brightest and darkest part of the picture) of about 50 to 1. On bright sunny days, when the contrast ratio can be 1000 to 1, or more, you need to decide which part of the scene has to be correctly exposed - usually the face. Then zoom in to the chosen feature, let the autoexposure find the right exposure and switch to manual. Or press the autoexposure lock button (if your camcorder has one).

Either way, when you zoom out again, the exposure on the face will stay correct. The light in other parts of the picture may be glaringly bright but this can be quite a pleasing effect.

If the light is directly behind the subject, the subject will be a silhouette. If the light is really bright, the subject will look like a black blob with fuzzy edges. This often happens if the subject is standing in front of a window and the daylight outside is much brighter than the artificial light inside.

There are various ways round the problem.

- **Avoid it**: close the curtains or position your subject against a different background.
- **Zoom in** to reduce the outdoor area in the picture.
- **Raise the camera** to reduce the area of sky in the picture.
- **Boost the artificial light** on your subject so that it matches the daylight.
- **Put a filter on the window(s)** to reduce the light coming in. (This will probably require more equipment, time and effort than you can manage if you're alone.)

Your camera may have a preset exposure to deal with excessive light behind the subject, called something like 'backlight compensation'. It may produce the exposure you want, but the autoexposure, back-to-manual technique is more reliable.

Of course, you might decide to accept the contrast and show your subject as a silhouette. This can look dramatic - for a time. But you can't expect viewers to watch and listen to a pitch-black cut-out for any length of time. Unless the cut-out is a spy or criminal or someone who has to stay anonymous.

Light that moves

If you pan across a scene, the light entering the camera may change very fast as the lens passes over a patch of sunlight or a bright window or a shiny surface. When the auto adjusts for light changes as sudden as these, the results are often unuseable. The brightness shoots up too far, overcorrects to too dark and then finds the right exposure, all in quick succession. Not pretty.

A ray of light reflected from a wristwatch, or headlamps sweeping across the lens can be enough to trigger these violent exposure swings. Ideally the autoexposure should ignore the changes. After all, you expect to be dazzled if you are caught in powerful headlamps.

The way to allow the camera to be dazzled is to lock the autoexposure. Or for more gentle light changes, use manual exposure to ride them.

Extras

Zebras

Some cameras highlight overexposed areas of the picture with black and white stripes - hence the name, zebras. You may be able to choose the brightness level for triggering zebras: anything from 60% to 100%. The zebras won't appear on the tape but you should reduce the exposure until they disappear, or almost disappear. Small areas of zebra may translate into acceptable highlights in the recorded picture.

Some people don't like using zebras, because they consider them over dominant in the viewfinder.

White balance and mixed light

We don't usually notice the colour of light. But daylight is in fact bluish and artificial light has an orange tinge. Our eyes and brain compensate for these variations so that skin tones and other colours look roughly the same indoors and out.

The white balance adjusts the camera for the prevailing colour of light. If the white balance is wrong, the colours on the recording will be wrong and the shots may be impossible to cut together with shots in which the balance is correct.

For scenes lit only by daylight or only by artificial light, you can use the auto white balance or the preset options built into the camera. For scenes with a mixture of daylight and artificial light, however, it's safer to set the white balance manually. To do this, light the scene you intend to shoot. Then put a sheet of white paper, or something white like a shirt (make sure it's truly white, not off-white) in the centre of the scene. Zoom in to fill frame with the white and adjust the exposure. Then press the white-balance button.

You should set the white balance at the start of every shoot and every time you move to a different source or mix of light. The camera will remember the setting so you don't need to repeat the procedure each time you switch off. But check that it retains the setting when you change batteries.

In some mixed-light scenes it may be impossible to find a satisfactory compromise for both types of light. In these situations it's usually more acceptable to let the daylight err towards blue and concentrate on the colours in the artificial light. the important thing is to get the skin tones right, particularly on faces. People watch faces and know the colours to expect. The colour of other things is less predictable.

The best way round the mixed-light problem is to eliminate it: switch off the artificial light or exclude daylight by closing the curtains. Or use filters, or lights that have the same colour temperature as daylight. But these solutions need more time, equipment and energy than you normally have when shooting solo.

Finally, you can usually correct faulty colours in the edit, but it takes time that would be better spent on the edit itself. As always, it's better to get things right when shooting rather than rely on rescues in the edit.

Shutter

This is not something you need worry about normally. But if you want to freeze fast-moving action or give slower-moving objects an attractive blur, read on.

Film cameras have a physical shutter that opens 24 times a second to expose each frame to the light. In a video camera the light-sensitive CCD chip(s) are always open to the light, but the intensity is 'read' and recorded only when the chip is scanned.

A video 'shutter' speed, therefore, depends on how many times the CCDs (imaging chips) are scanned each second: 50 times in the UK and 60 in the US (the electricity supplies differ). In other words, the video shutter speed is 1/50 of a second in the UK and 1/60 in the US. These speeds can produce a slight blur if something in the picture moves, but this blur doesn't usually matter. At 24 fps (for film) or 25 fps (for video) viewers see the blurs as seamless motion (fps = frames per second).

If you want to view a frame as a still, the blur matters, particularly if you shoot ultrafast action such as a racing car or jet aircraft at the normal shutter speed. This is where faster shutter speeds come into their own. If you shoot, say, 1000 frames a second (1/1000) - possible only in bright conditions - each individual frame should be fast enough to 'freeze' the action and give you a sharp still.

If you play back your 1000 fps shots as moving pictures, however, the sequence will look jerky. This is because playback speed is always 25 fps, however fast the shutter speed. Viewers see only 25 of the 1000 frames taken each second. The ultrafast cars and aircraft travel an appreciable distance in the unseen 24 frames between each frame viewed.

Sometimes jerky playback doesn't matter. You might, for example, record your tennis serve or golf swing with a faster shutter speed to spot mistakes. Try viewing the results both as stills and in slow motion.

Slower than normal shutter speeds - 1/6 or 1/12 of a second - produce blurry pictures that can be attractive as a special effect. They might be just right for shooting a dance or dream sequence, or drunken fantasies.

Finally, you may find that you can stop computer screens flickering in shot by using a faster shutter speed.

On-board light

The light built in (or on) your camera is a rough and ready way of brightening up the picture but it isn't artistic. Its throw is limited, so if the subject is distant it won't make any difference. If the subject is too close, the colours will look washed out, the background may be unnaturally dark or there may be a big, black shadow on the wall behind. The problem is that the on-board light illuminates head-on (like car headlamps) and lighting usually looks better when it's coming from the side.

Stand-alone lights and safety

A stand-alone light avoids the headlamp effect, but it's another thing to lug around and set up. If you are thinking of using more than one light, you need someone to help, preferably a qualified electrician. It's easy to put too many lights on a circuit and blow a fuse. The lights can get very hot and set things on fire. If someone trips over a stand or cable, the light can topple over and cause serious injury. And don't forget the porter problem: who is going to carry them between car and location?

Reflectors

A white umbrella or a fold-up reflector can be used to reflect any light that is available on location. These offer a more practical option for the solo operator, being lighter to carry around, quicker to set up, and not having the same safety risks. They can be very effective if you want to give a gentle lift to shadows.

Exercises

- Shoot:
  in bright light
  against the light
  in high contrast situations
  in low light
  in candlelight
  Watch what happens to focus in all these situations.

- Move from artificial to natural light and vice versa.

- Experiment with gain and different shutter speeds.

Sound

Pictures sell cameras, sound doesn't. Manufacturers invest in picture acquisition and skimp on sound, so you may have to buy extra equipment to get good sound. The extra investment will be worth it; in many types of programme the sound carries most of the information. Viewers will put up with poor pictures. They give up on poor sound.

Essentials

On-board microphone

Be wary of the on-board microphone. It records general sound on a location satisfactorily, but it may also pick up camera noise, particularly from the zoom motor. You may have to avoid zooming when using the on-board mic.

It may also record sound from your handling of the camera, the lens cap clicking against the camera casing, and any remarks you mutter to yourself when your eye is pressed against the viewfinder. You are further away from the mic when viewing the shot on the monitor screen. But even then, be careful with hand movements on the camera and no comments, please.

Any wind on the mic also leaves its mark - a close-up, rasping noise that will make the recording unusable. Use the wind gag or wind screen if there is one; also try and shelter the camera from direct gusts. A person with their back to the wind and holding their coat open can be effective. Even better, if you have a spare person with you, get him or her to hold a separate mic closer to the action.

Monitoring levels

The camera automatically adjusts the volume level of the on-board mic This works for most situations but there are occasions when it works against you. In a restaurant, for example, during pauses in a conversation or interview, the auto will boost background buzz, hums, whirrs, clanking of cutlery and crockery - noises that should stay in the background. In other situations it may reduce the level of sounds that you want to keep loud, such as fortissimo moments in music, or an audience applauding and cheering. On such occasions it's better not to use the auto.

Setting levels manually, however, can be fiddly and time-consuming. You will also need to monitor them, with a good set of headphones and an eye on the screen display.

If you are using more than one external mic it's worth investing in a sound mixer (that's a piece of equipment) to adjust the levels. A sound recordist (that's a person) who can take all these problems off your hands is an even better investment. (Don't forget, going solo means you are trying to get good pictures and direct the action as well.)

Interviews

For most interviews the on-board mic may be OK, if there isn't too much surrounding noise and the person talking is fairly close (not more than about a metre and a half away). For more reliable quality, however, you need to choose a different mic A rifle (or gun) mic is highly directional (it has a narrow pick-up angle) and when pointed accurately and positioned close to the interviewee gives excellent results. It's sensitive to wind noise, so use it with a windshield.

A personal (or lapel) mic clipped to the interviewee's clothes (remember to tuck the cable out of sight) has advantages for the solo operator. It's tiny (less hardware to carry around), easier to position and also comes with a windshield. But although unobtrusive, it's not suitable for dramatic situations where you want viewers to forget they are watching TV and become caught up in the action.

If the interviewee has to move round while talking, the cable linking the personal mic to the camera becomes a hindrance. The solution is to use a personal mic with a radio transmitter - a radio mic

If interviewee and interviewer need to move unencumbered, two radio mics are the most convenient solution. Record questions and answers on different tracks. You can then optimise the levels during postproduction.

Before you set out to do an interview, work out which mics you need, remind yourself how to connect and operate them and do a test recording. Using add-on mics may take more time and be more complicated than you expect. They may, for example, need to be switched on separately and have their own batteries, which have a habit of running out at critical moments.

Extras

More options mean more complication. To get the full benefit of things like stereo and digital you have to go into a lot of technical detail and, realistically speaking, you can no longer go solo.

Once again you really need an extra pair of hands - a sound recordist.

Exercises

- Find out how to connect and use the on-board mic and any external mics you have.

- Find out the best way to monitor sound levels. Can you play back audio on location to check it?

- Which of these does the on-board mic pick up?
  Changing your grip on the camera?
  Operating the power or manual zooms?
  Talking to yourself behind the camera?
  Wind? Test by fanning or blowing on the mic from various distances.

- Test your mics in different locations to get a feel for their areas of acceptance:
  Somewhere quiet with a low hum in the background.
  In a busy road pointing to and away from traffic.
  How does the auto level control behave in these situations?

- Finally, experiment to find the best way of doing an interview in the same locations.

Time code

Time code (TC) is a labelling and tracking system that is convenient for humans and indispensable for machines. It assigns a different 8 digit number to every frame: for example, 00:02:45:14. The left-hand pair of digits can be used for the cassette number or date or whatever you choose; the next pair records minutes; the next, seconds; and the final pair, frames.

There are two main types of TC: **rec(ord) run** and **free run**. You need to choose the one that is best for your type of programme.

Rec-run TC

The camera will automatically put down continuous TC if it's in the rec-run mode, the default mode and, on some cameras, the only TC mode.

There may, however, be a TC gap if you change batteries or eject a cassette and put it back again. To avoid this, press the end-search or return button after the change. This ensures that the camera picks up and continues the TC from the previous shot.

Free-run TC

The other TC mode is 'free run' or 'time of day'. This labels each frame with the time, taken from a clock built into the camera - check that it's set correctly. The clock keeps running even if you aren't shooting, so every time you stop recording and restart, the TC will jump.

Free-run TC is useful for long, continuous events that you are recording mainly for the highlights, like goals in a football match or sound bites in a speech. Jot down the time anything interesting happens, so that you can go straight to it during the edit.

Free-run TC is also useful at conferences. If you are shooting with - say - three cameras, make sure their clocks all show the same time. It's easy then for the editor to find the same moment on the recordings and cut between the chairman on camera one, audience reaction on two, and the wide shot of the committee walking out on three.

Salvaging TC

To edit videotape accurately you need a continuous sequence of TC numbers without breaks or repetitions.

What happens if you don't have continuous TC on your cassettes? All is not lost, but all is not convenient either.

When you transfer your material into the edit machine (known as capturing or digitising) you can let the machine write its own TC to the material, ignoring the TC on original cassette.

This leaves you with another problem. When you finish editing, you may want to use the edit decision list (EDL) to make a full-strength copy from the original cassettes (an operation known as rendering or conforming). But the TC on the edit won't match the TC on the original cassettes.

To avoid this, you have to take action before the edit. Copy all the original cassettes onto new cassettes with new continuous TC and then treat these copies as the originals - in other words, use them for both capturing and conforming. You don't have to worry about losing quality. With digital technology, all copies are exact copies (clones) of the originals and picture quality isn't affected. But there is a cost: cloning takes time and you have to pay for another set of cassettes.

VITC and LTC

You may also come across the initials VITC (Vertical Interval Time Code) and LTC (Longitudinal Time Code).

The important distinction between these two is that LTC displays a TC only when the edit machine is running.

User bits

Some cameras also offer a second set of eight-digit numbers known as user bits. You can use these to record information such as the camera settings, the date and time, and the scene and take numbers.

How much you use them depends on how easy it is to access the (often tiny) controls and how nimble your fingers are.

Technical matters

Wide screen

If you record using the wide-screen option, your pictures will fill a 16:9 screen (16 units wide by 9 units high). If you play back a wide-screen recording on a 4:3 screen, depending on the mode you choose, your pictures will appear either with a 'letter box' (a black band above and below) or compressed. You won't be able get back to a full-screen picture on a 4:3 screen.

Other effects

Your camera will offer you all sorts of other effects: fade-ins and fade-outs, slow motion, freeze frames, mirror images and so on. Explore them - they're fun.

But avoid using them when you are shooting. Once they are recorded, you can't get rid of them. If you want effects, introduce them during the edit. You can then fine-tune exactly as you want. Or decide not to use them.

Holes in the picture

If you find little rectangular holes or gaps in the recorded picture, there's probably dust or dirt on the recording heads.

The problem is visible only on playback, so watch carefully when you review shots in the viewfinder or monitor screen. The camera may display a flashing icon to warn you about the problem. Briefly running a cleaning cassette may help, but - more likely - the camera will have to go for repair.

Tape creases

Loading and unloading cassettes can crease or stretch the tape. So don't park or eject cassettes halfway through usable material.

And don't rewind cassettes in the camera immediately after recording. It wastes time and batteries. Wait till you get back to base.

Electricity

Be wary of strong electrical or magnetic fields: they may affect a recording or even damage the camera. Near power cables, transmitters, aluminium factories, radar and such like, ask where it's safe to shoot.

Camera care

Temperature

Excessive heat and cold can damage cameras and batteries. Don't leave them in direct sunlight, especially in a car.

Sudden temperature changes are also unwelcome. If you take a cold camera into a humid environment such as a heated swimming pool, moisture will condense on (and possibly in) the camera. Bad news. To avoid this, seal the camera in a plastic bag and leave it to warm up slowly somewhere safe in the heated area. This may take 30 minutes or more. Use this time to unpack the other equipment, plan the shoot and drink coffee.

Water

Your camera won't like getting wet. Protect it with an umbrella when it's raining and buy the custom-made rain jacket if you are going to do a lot of all-weather shooting.

Keep the camera away from seawater and spray. In humid climates keep equipment as dry as possible by storing it in plastic bags with silica gel sachets to soak up the moisture.

If the camera does get damp (there may be a warning light) take out the cassette and leave the cradle open for about an hour. If you also leave it running (use mains power), the heat from the motor will help dry it out.

Sand

Very bad news. If sand gets into the works, the camera will have to be professionally cleaned and even then it may be a write-off.

On beaches or in deserts never put a camera on the sand. If the sand is blowing about, keep the camera out of the wind or in the rain jacket. Dusty places, like flour mills, can also be harmful.

If sand gets onto the monitor screen or lens, use a blower brush or a lens cleaning cloth (gently). Don't use your finger.

Rough handling

Obviously knocks, bumps and vibrations are bad for the camera. Make sure it can't roll about on short trips in the car. For longer journeys and bumpy roads keep it in its case.

Don't throw the case around when loading and unloading.

Wobbly shots

The best way to get wobble-free shots is to use the standard good-practice techniques below. They will reduce and probably eliminate most camera shake, even if you don't have any extra equipment.

Reducing wobbles

1　Don't use the narrow-angle end of the zoom. It exaggerates wobbles. Instead shoot as much as you can with the lens zoomed out. This reduces apparent wobbling. Stay close to the subject so that he, she or it isn't lost in the picture.

2　Rest the camera on something solid, like a wall or gate or car or on the ground. If you can't steady the camera, steady yourself by propping your elbows on one of the aforementioned. Or lean against something.

3　Failing a support, you can eliminate most wobbles by standing with your legs slightly apart and holding the camera with both hands. If you want to pan, keep the top half of the body steady and move from the hips.

4　For a walking shot do a Groucho Marx walk: crab-like, with your legs a little bent. This minimises movement in the top half of the body.

5　Use the above techniques even if you are using the built-in image stabiliser (called steadishot or something similar). Stabilisers smooth out wobbles rather than eliminate them. So they need all the help you can give them. Experiment with the stabiliser in your camera. How much camera shake can it cope with? Are shots steadier with it switched off (worth checking)? What happens if you zoom in and then do a slow pan?

6　The steadying techniques described above will produce acceptable shots for things that are moving. Unless the camera is resting on something solid (see point 2 above) they won't give steady shots for a static subject, particularly if the subject is in close-up. Signs and notice boards, for example, don't move, so they make even the most steady handheld shots look shaky.

Reducing wobbles with extra equipment

1   **Tripod** The trouble with tripods is that they are another thing to carry. It's tempting to try and get by without one, but in some situations (such as a press conference or lecture) and for some shots (locked-off or time lapse), a tripod is essential.

Make sure yours has a good panning and tilting head, telescopic legs that are easy to use, and a quick-release lever to part the tripod from the camera. The screw mount is useless when you want to go handheld in a hurry.

2   **Monopod** A one-legged tripod (a monopod) with a carrying strap that goes over the shoulder is lighter than a tripod and simple to use. Worth considering.

3   **Shoulder mount** This keeps the camera perched on your shoulder like a parrot and is a useful piece of kit, if you are going solo on long shoots and need a free hand to make notes or move equipment. Check if there is one for your camera.

4   Make sure the built-in **image stabiliser** is switched on. This smooths out minor wobbles by comparing each frame with the one that went before and minimising the change. The more advanced systems are programmed to recognise deliberate moves like pans and will not try to correct them.

5   **Steadicam** This is the expensive solution to the camera shake problem and once you've got the hang of it, gives you beautifully smooth moving shots. The drawback is getting in and out of the harness and wearing it for long periods, which can be tiring and strain your back. A handheld stabiliser may be a more practical solution.

Finally

You may decide to adopt wobbly shooting as a 'style'. You won't be the first person to do this. The trouble is, can you think of a single film or programme where you can honestly say that the wobbles improved the content?

Camera shake and wobble may give an authentic look to riots or chase sequences, but if you use them as the style for a complete film, you'll lose more admirers than you gain.

Safety and security

Safety on page 30 discusses the dangers faced by all programme-makers and refers you to two invaluable websites: *www.bbc-safety.co.uk* and *www.shootingpeople.org*.

Going solo is inherently more dangerous than working with a crew. Your judgement may suffer because of all the things on your mind and the pressure that piles up on you to get everything done. There's no second opinion to restrain you and you start to take risks that you normally wouldn't dream of.

Accidents and emergencies don't leave you alone because you are alone.

Before the shoot

1   Make a realistic assessment of the risks of a shoot before you go. Many organisations insist that you submit a written assessment before you set off. Are you sufficiently insured?

2   Don't be tempted to pretend to be a tourist to make a programme in hostile countries. You could be endangering others as well as yourself. What may happen to your local contacts and any programme-makers who may follow you?

3   Always give a colleague at base details and phone numbers of the contacts you are planning to meet and the time you expect to get back.

4   Discuss also the procedures you will both follow if you don't check in or arrive back at the agreed time. Both of you should have a written copy of the plan.

5   What if you go home directly after the shoot? Make provision for this in your plan.

6   On foreign shoots you should check in with base by phone or email at least once a day to update on progress and give details of your plans.

7   Always carry an ID card and a letter on headed notepaper from your manager or parent organisation saying what you are doing and why.

8   If you are knocking unannounced on people's doors, don't assume a warm welcome. Your subjects may have had a hard time with previous programme-makers. They may be keen to get their own back and, as far as they are concerned, you are just one more member of the tormenting media. You shouldn't be going on shoots like this alone.

Equipment

1   Your equipment is worth a lot of money. Don't leave it unattended in public areas. Put the stuff you aren't using into a rucksack and keep it on your back. Be realistic about how much gear you can carry at the same time as doing the job.

2   Taking gear to dodgy areas at night (or even during the day) is not a good idea, even in a rucksack. If you have to take this sort of risk, you must take someone to accompany you. For criminals two people make a more difficult target than one.

3   Keep loose cash in a pocket and the rest (as little as possible) somewhere else. If someone decides he wants all your money, hand it over. It's not worth fighting for.

4   In non-threatening places like an office or department store, you can take more gear with you. Keep it in a trolley or - better, because it hides the contents - in a bag on wheels.

On the shoot

1   Never do a shot walking backwards without someone guiding you. Tripping on a kerb or falling off the edge of a pavement can have serious consequences.

2   Cables, lighting stands and equipment cases can also cause trips and falls. Unused equipment lying around is easy to steal.

3   When you are shooting, the viewfinder lures you into a dream/screen-world, where it's easy to think of yourself as a detached, invisible observer immune from danger, even when you can see the danger in the shot. Beware 'bubble' thinking.

4   You may be even more at risk from things that you can't see in the viewfinder. In danger areas use the monitor screen, which lets you look around while shooting. Look round regularly.

5   If things get really dangerous, leave. Discretion is better than disaster.

6   Don't forget to check in with base as planned.

7   When you read this, relaxed and unstressed, it all sounds a bit extreme. When you are absorbed in shooting, however, your awareness of danger is much reduced. Think safety.

After the shoot

1   Don't forget, tiredness makes you careless. How many hours, including travel time, have you been on the go? How likely are you to do something stupid because you're exhausted?

2   The drive back is often the most dangerous part of the job. You're tired, you relax and you don't feel the need to concentrate as much. You think it's all over...

Solo directing

Before you can fill the director's role you have to master operating the camera. Practise until it's second nature. What will contributors think if you keep referring to the manual?

Directors direct contributors and the crew. If there is no crew to whom to explain the story, you may not actually know what it is. Your film, however, still needs a story, an approach to telling it, a list of contributors, locations and potential sequences, an understanding of their relative importance and how long to spend on each.

Don't think you can improvise this on the hoof, while you are shooting. As a one-man band you will have less time to think, so you need more preparation, not less. Research and recce, treatment and storyboard, which events to cover when and where, interview objectives and so on – the better you prepare, the better your results are likely to be.

If you are on a rush job and don't have time to prepare, at least think about what the finished film may look like. You then have an idea of what you might get, if you're lucky. Jot down the sequences. In the excitement of the shoot it's easy to forget crucial bits, so refer to the list before you pack up on location.

If you are working for a regional programme or planning a shoot abroad, does your story have a local connection? The world may be a global village but programme editors still love a local or national angle (as is evident in programmes that travel to the ends of the earth to interview a fellow countryman).

One of the advantages of going solo is that you can take the camera with you on recces and shoot those telling incidents that can't be repeated on request. 'If only I'd had the camera with me...' Now you can. Before you unpack the camera, however, make sure that your subjects don't mind you taking some 'preparatory' shots.

Use the camera to speed up note-taking. Take shots of business cards, name plates etc. to record how your subjects' names are spelled, and their correct work titles. It's quicker than writing in a notebook.

Should I go solo?

Advantages

1   Solo is cheaper. Only one person needs funding on location.

2   Solo is democratic. Before camcorders, newcomers to the industry were slotted into production or technical roles. Now everyone can be director and technician.

3   Solo is unobtrusive. A crew is always outside the action, looking in. A solo operator can be inside the action.

4   Making a solo programme is an ideal way to get into the industry. It shows commitment and what you are capable of.

5   Solo is suitable for many types of programme:
  • Low budget.
  • Quick turn-round journalism.
  • Programmes in cramped places like cars.
  • Video diaries and DIY.
  • Fly-on-the-wall.
  • Archaeology digs or wild life, where things don't happen to schedule.
  • Programmes that wouldn't otherwise get made.
  • Foreign trips beyond the normal programme budget.

Disadvantages

1   There's no-one to park the car, help carry the equipment, do the sound, guard the gear and watch your back.

2   There's no-one to discuss things with or get ideas from or give a second opinion. Crews get a lot more shooting experience than directors and you can't tap into that experience.

3   You are unlikely to be equally interested or talented in all aspects of programme-making: developing ideas, handling contributors, picture composition, shooting, recording sound, interviewing, editing, graphics, script writing and more.

4   Technology gets better, but how good are you at using it? The specialists use it all the time. It's no surprise if they use it better and faster.

Index